energy

Fourth in the Sierra Club Battlebook Series

energy

A crisis in power

by John Holdren and Philip Herrera

Sierra Club   San Francisco • New York

The Sierra Club, founded in 1892 by
John Muir, has devoted itself to the study
and protection of the nation's scenic and
ecological resources—mountains, wetlands,
woodlands, wild shores and rivers. All
club publications are part of the nonprofit
effort the club carries on as a public trust.
There are 37 chapters coast to coast, in
Canada, Hawaii and Alaska. Participation
is invited in the club's program to enjoy and
preserve wilderness everywhere. Address:
1050 Mills Tower, San Francisco, California
94104; 250 West 57th Street, New York,
N.Y. 10019, or 235 Massachusetts Avenue
N.E., Washington, D.C. 20002.

This battlebook is printed on Valentine
Precycle Offset. The paper is manufactured
from a nonwood fiber called bagasse.
Bagasse is the residue that remains after
sucrose has been extracted from sugar cane.
The environmental benefits of using Precycle
Offset are multiple: bagasse traditionally is
burned (causing air pollution) or used for
landfill in the wetlands of the Southeast.
Second printing, January 1973.

Copyright © 1971 by the Sierra Club.
All rights reserved.
Library of Congress catalog card number
78-177949.
International Standard Book number
87156-055-0.

Designed and produced by Charles Curtis,
Inc., New York, and printed in the United
States of America by Grafix.

Project Coordinator: Peter Borrelli

Contents

Contents
(continued)

Introduction

Where were *you* when the lights went out? Most of us living in or around New York during the 1965 blackout have rather vivid memories of Fun City's famous power failure. Others will never forget it for the embarrassment it caused the industry. For those concerned with defending the environment, the big blackout has assumed symbolic importance. It raised a laundry list of questions about environmental quality, technological reliability, consumer protection, and both corporate and governmental responsibility. Subsequent blackouts and brownouts, together with the continuing disappearance of green, open spaces and the steady deterioration of our nation's air and water, have brought home the fact that the energy providing our heat, light and power is largely gained by chemical destruction of nonrenewable resources.

We are without question in the midst of what has been popularly termed—frequently in the vain hope of wishing it away—an "energy crisis." The crisis is characterized by numerous, interrelated, unanswered questions about the future of America's environment, resources, technology, economy, national priorities and policy. And contrary to popular belief, the crisis is neither the invention of environmental fadists nor a fantasy of gloomy prophets. It is very real. And it has been a long time in the making, beginning with the invention of the steam engine and the rise of the industrial revolution.

Our civilization and economy have been built upon a prodigious consumption of energy—energy derived mostly from the burning of fossil fuels. Virtually all of the benefits that now seem necessary to the "American way" have required vast amounts of energy. Energy, in short, has been our ultimate raw material, for our commitment to economic growth has also been a commitment to the use of steadily increasing amounts of energy necessary to the production of goods and services.

The extraction, transportation and preparation of fuels; the manufacture of energy conversion machinery; the production of electric power, and the management of waste products and waste heat are industrial activities which have grown exponentially in the past few decades. The rate of growth has been so rapid that knowledgeable observers are beginning to question whether we should allow it to continue shaping public policy and economic behavior. Forecasts based on extrapolations of energy consumption, population growth rates, and anticipated changes in human behavior, though generally conservative, seem unrealistic: growth now reveals limits imposed by environmental factors. Recognition of the finite capability of air and water and landscape to yield fuels and to assimilate wastes, therefore, poses a direct challenge to growth.

"Our society," notes author Ralph Lapp, "can no longer tolerate a laissez-faire attitude toward energy. Prudent policy requires that we consider not just the physical problems of reserves, conservation and pollution; we need to inquire into the legitimacy of our future energy demands . . ." And he adds: "Our energy affluence is not at an end, but it is clearly approaching a crossroad unmarked by signposts, except one —CAUTION."

The most dramatic and direct challenge to the increasing

consumption of energy has emerged from confrontation between the electric utility industry and environmentalists. During the past decade the average growth rate of energy consumption in all its forms has been more than 4 percent annually, but the growth of electric power consumption has been particularly phenomenal. Increasing at a rate of about 7 percent annually in recent years, electric power is expected to double every ten years, representing perhaps 50 percent of total U.S. energy consumption by the year 2000. The industry, operating on a system of conventional economics and short-term objectives, is hard pressed to meet this demand. Environmentalists likewise feel pressed. Thus, the confrontation.

But as yet most lawmakers and regulatory bodies are stymied by the simultaneous clamor for more power and a better environment. Largely unresponsive to the dynamics of social forces, they have become as immovable as the electric power industry itself (the nation's largest industry in terms of capital investments in facilities). Which leads one to ask, Who's defending the public interest? Answer: No one. Or at least no one whose primary responsibility it is.

As a result, legions of informed citizens have emerged to defend their own rights. Critical of institutionalized decision making, they have created new forums, forced others to be more responsive, and discovered and dusted off a wide array of democratic weaponry. Their battle cries come from a growing list of campaigns—Bodega Bay, Turkey Point, Storm King, Palisades, Calvert Cliffs—which have demonstrated forcefully the role and effectiveness of the citizen in defending the environment and in determining public policy. Each case further demonstrates that at this time the public interest in seeking a diminution of environmental degradation is, in the words of one California jurist, "an overriding public interest which must stand paramount and supreme when contrasted with the public interest (of residents) in obtaining all the electric power they desire."

In the following pages John Holdren, physicist at the University of California's Lawrence Livermore Laboratory, and Philip Herrera, environment editor of *Time* magazine, carefully and thoughtfully examine the problems of energy, electric power and the environment. They offer, respectively, a scientist's overview essential to an understanding of America's most visible—and vocal—environmental issue, and a journalist's account of a remarkable effort by concerned citizens to protect the environment. Together, the authors' observations and recommendations can advance us toward a rational energy policy for the United States—and perhaps a solution to a crisis that already affects the life of every citizen.

Peter Borrelli
New York, N.Y.
Sepember, 1971

Part one

Energy: resources and consumption

by John Holdren

1. Understanding Energy

Trends in energy use;
forecasts of future consumption;
the crisis.

Ask a scientist to define energy and you are likely to get a lecture rather than a simple answer. For although energy plays a dominant role in our science, our society, and the processes of life itself, it is readily described only in terms of what it does, rather than what it is. Nobel Laureate Richard Feynman, in his celebrated *Lectures on Physics**, calls energy "a numerical quantity which does not change when something happens." His definition refers to the law of conservation of energy, which says that energy is neither created nor destroyed but only changes in form. For most of our purposes here, we shall settle for a less comprehensive but more practical definition: "Energy is the capacity to do work."

The work it does is the operation of the biosphere and the maintenance of agricultural and industrial civilization. Radiant energy flowing from the sun warms the earth to life-sustaining temperatures, drives the hydrological cycle of evaporation and precipitation, powers the winds and ocean currents, and is captured by photosynthesis to fuel the earth's

---

*Italicized titles refer to bibliography at the end of Part I.

biota. Of the solar energy reaching the surface of the earth, roughly one-tenth of 1 percent is utilized by photosynthesis—two-thirds on land and one-third in the seas. Of this amount, in turn, the metabolic requirements of man and his livestock account for roughly 1 percent. In a system of some millions of species, of course, the appropriation of a percent of the biological energy flow to serve the needs of only one species is a remarkable feat. Ecologists find this situation disturbing as well as remarkable, because they know that the stability of ecological systems, including those that support mankind, is related to the balanced flow of energy through the widest variety of biological pathways.

Man's use of energy far exceeds his metabolic requirements, however. Historically, his population and his material wealth have grown in step with his ability to harness inanimate energy—first as wood and wind, later as falling water and fossil fuels, finally as the energy of the nucleus. The first four categories represent stored solar energy in different forms. The fifth, nuclear energy, originated when the constituents that eventually became our sun and its planets were fused together from elemental hydrogen in more distant stars. Today, man is mobilizing and consuming energy from these various stored sources at a rate some fifteen times that of his metabolic consumption, and three times that of the combined metabolic consumption of him and his livestock. It is this prodigious use of inanimate energy—its history, the nature of the fuels and the technologies that sustain it, and the implications of present trends—which will concern us here.

We shall find that formulating a rational strategy for energy use requires definitive analysis of a host of questions that have only recently begun to be taken seriously. Is personal well-being—"standard of living," if you will—as directly related to per capita energy consumption as the energy promoters would have us believe? (Obviously there is a connection, up to a point, but the United States as a whole may be well beyond it.) What fraction of today's spiraling energy demand is actually being used to satisfy the undisputed needs of the poor, whose plight is so often held out as an excuse for technological exercises of little relevance to them? How much of the legitimate demand arising from a certain unavoidable amount of population growth, and from the aspirations of the impoverished to a decent existence, can be met by cutting back on frivolous and wasteful uses of energy by the affluent, rather than by increasing production?

In a hypothetical world, free of the constraints of biology and thermodynamics, such thorny, socioeconomic questions might not have to be asked at all; the energy problem would be reduced to the technical details of meeting any demand that happened to materialize. Unfortunately, we do not live in such a world. Energy is not merely the prime mover of technology; it is also a central ingredient in man's impact on his environment. No means of supplying energy is without liabilities, and no form of its consumption is without consequence to the ecosystems that support us.

Thus, burning fossil fuels pollutes the air, defaces the landscape, and depletes a resource ultimately needed for other uses—lubrication, synthesis, perhaps protein culture. Fission reactors generate a burden of radioactive wastes which must be infallibly contained, unerringly transported, and indefinitely interred. Hydroelectric sites are in limited supply, and exploiting them has aesthetic and ecological drawbacks. Solar energy is unevenly distributed in space and time, dilute, and correspondingly expensive to harness. Controlled thermonuclear fusion has not yet been conclusively demonstrated to be technologically feasible, nor can anyone say with assurance what it will cost when we get it. This list does not exhaust the possibilities for energy sources, nor does it include all the defects of the ones named. But it serves to suggest that there are no easy solutions to the so-called "energy crisis." The details that follow will not change this conclusion.

Thermodynamics and Terminology

Understanding energy problems in depth requires a passing acquaintance with the principles of thermodynamics and with the terminology and units of measurement associated with energy and power. First of all, energy and power are not the same thing. If energy is defined as the capacity to do work, then power is the rate at which work is done or, equivalently, the rate at which energy is consumed.

Unfortunately, these simple definitions can get us into difficulty. The law of conservation of energy, also called the first law of thermodynamics, says that energy cannot actually be consumed at all. Thus, when we say energy is consumed, we really mean it is changed in form. The second law of thermodynamics, in turn, says that such changes proceed in such a way as to reduce, on the whole, the availability of energy to do work. In other words, the usefulness of energy is effectively consumed, even though the energy is still present in one form or another. Energy that has been changed in form with a reduction in usefulness—that is, capacity to do work—is said to have been *degraded.* For example, in doing the work that makes light, most of the electrical energy passing through a light bulb is degraded to heat. The light energy itself may do work and be degraded to heat upon being absorbed.

Energy can also be transformed in the opposite direction, from less useful to more useful form, but only at the expense of degrading a fraction of the initial amount of energy present. Such processes are called *energy conversion,* and the generation of electricity is one example. Here, the useful heat energy released, say, in the burning of fossil fuel is partly converted into electrical energy of higher usefulness and partly degraded into relatively useless low-temperature heat. (The words "temperature" and "heat" are not interchangeable: heat is a form of energy, and temperature is a measure of the usefulness of that heat. The higher the temperature, the more useful the heat.)

The real message of the second law of thermodynamics, then, is that energy, unlike most resources, cannot be recycled. The total availability, or capacity to do work, in a given amount of energy can be used only once. Even in energy conversion, when all aspects of the process are considered, the total availability of the energy involved has gone irretrievably downhill. Thus the laws of thermodynamics have sometimes been stated this way: the first law says you can't win; the second law says you can't break even and you can't get out of the game.

Power has a broader meaning than simply the rate at which work is done. It is the rate at which energy is processed, where processing can mean conversion, degradation, the performance of useful work, or even simply transmission. It is helpful to write this definition as an equation:

$$\text{power} = \frac{\text{amount of energy processed}}{\text{length of time during which processing occurs}},$$

or, rearranged more tersely, energy = power x time. Note that energy is the more fundamental of the two quantities. If we have a gallon of gasoline, we have a specified amount of energy; but the power we produce when we burn it can be anything, depending on how *fast* we do so. The gallon might produce 50 horsepower for half an hour in your automobile, or 60,000 horsepower for a second and a half in a Boeing 747.

Unfortunately for laymen and specialists alike, the wealth of material that has been written concerning energy and power is cluttered with a confusing array of units for the measurement of these quantities—for example, British thermal units (BTU) for the energy content of fuels, kilocalories (kcal, or Cal) for the energy content of foods, kilowatt-hours for amounts of electrical energy. However, one set of units can as well be used for all applications, and relationships are made much clearer by doing so. We shall use the kilowatt-hour as our basic unit for measuring energy. Since it contains a unit of power (kilowatt) and a unit of time (hour), its use as the fundamental unit of energy serves as a reminder of the relation connecting these three quantities. This all-purpose unit is usually denoted *kilowatt-hour (thermal),* abbreviated kwht, to distinguish it from the more specialized unit of electrical energy, the kilowatt-hour (electrical), abbreviated kwhe. The corresponding units of power, kilowatt (thermal) and kilowatt (electrical), are abbreviated kwt and kwe.*

Trends in Energy Use. The use of energy in the United States during the past two decades and indeed the past century has been characterized by three central features: enormous growth, major shifts in the relative importance of competing sources, and significant changes in the patterns of consumption (most notably the increasing use of electricity). These features have been tightly interrelated: new uses for energy have stimulated growth and, in turn, been stimulated by it; rising demand has prompted innovation to provide a matching supply, and innovation and competition have kept costs falling, which stimulated still further increases in demand. It has been taken as an article of faith in the energy industries that all these factors will continue to operate in the future as they have in the past—that competing new technologies will drive the cost of energy ever lower, and that the economy will respond by using even more of it per capita. Actually, there are good reasons for believing this will not be the case, and—at least in the United States—there are compelling reasons for working to prevent it. These reasons will unfold as we examine the energy picture in detail. A logical starting point is a closer look at the trends that have been operative up to the present.

The consumption of inanimate energy in the United States during the period 1880 to 1969, broken down by sources, is shown in Figure 1. Two surges of growth are evident, separated by a slack period between 1920 and 1940. During the first surge, from 1880 to 1920, the average rate of increase in consumption was 3.5 percent per year, which corresponds to a doubling time of twenty years.** In the second surge, consumption doubled between 1940 and 1965; the rate of growth itself has been increasing since then. The

---

*One kwht equals 3,412 BTU or 860 kcal. One kwt equals 1.34 horsepower. A ton of good coal yields 7,400 kwht, a barrel of crude oil 1,660 kwht, a thousand cubic feet of natural gas 315 kwht.
**The time for a quantity to double at a compound growth rate of 3.5 percent per year is approximately 70÷3.5 years.

5.1 percent increase observed between 1968 and 1969 would lead, if it persisted, to additional doublings of U.S. energy consumption every fourteen years. As is shown in Figure 1, total consumption in 1969 was over 19 trillion kwht*, or almost thirteen times the 1880 figure. This 1969 U.S. consumption, incidentally, amounted to just over one-third of the energy consumed in the entire world during that year.

Almost as remarkable as this phenomenal growth itself is the shifting composition of energy sources that sustained it. In 1880, more than half the total was supplied by fuel wood and nearly all the rest by coal. By 1900, fuel wood's share had dropped to 20 percent; oil, natural gas, and hydropower had appeared on the scene to claim 10 percent of the market among them; and coal accounted for the remaining 70 percent. Between 1900 and 1920 the fossil fuels increased their combined share to 90 percent; they have maintained and even slightly increased that dominant position up to the present. However, whereas the bulk of the growth in energy consumption from 1880 to 1940 was fueled by coal, the liquid and gaseous fossil fuels have absorbed the brunt of the increase since then.

Nuclear energy, barely visible on the chart with one-quarter of 1 percent of total energy consumption in 1969, is expected by many to provide the next major revolution in the composition of energy supply. Such a shift, however, is unlikely to be as rapid as either the displacement of fuel wood by coal or the displacement of coal by oil and natural gas. A major reason is that the contribution of nuclear energy today is restricted to the electrical component of the energy budget, and is likely to be so for some time. Nuclear reactors will probably remain impractical or uneconomical for most applications requiring a portable energy source. Their use as a source of raw heat for industrial processes does not seem imminent.

In recent years, electricity has received the lion's share of the public attention focused on energy problems, although

---

*One trillion = 1,000,000,000,000 = one thousand billion.

it accounts for less than 25 percent of U.S. energy consumption. As a "secondary" energy source, electricity is derived in all cases from one or the other of the "primary" sources, these being the fossil fuels, nuclear fuels, falling water, and —to a presently unimportant extent—tidal, geothermal, wind and direct solar energy. The use of electricity is increasing considerably faster than total energy consumption—since 1940 it has been doubling roughly every ten years—which accounts for the intense interest in electric power in general and nuclear power in particular. Even if the recent, dramatic growth rates were to persist, however, electricity would not account for 50 percent of total U.S. energy use until about 2015. Nor is it really meaningful to consider electricity in isolation from other uses of the primary energy sources, because much of the growth of electricity consumption occurs when electricity is substituted for direct use of the fuels themselves.

Forecasts of Future Energy Consumption

A forecast is not the same thing as a prediction. A prediction means we think we know what will happen at some time in the future. A forecast is a much more cautious thing. It says that *if* a variety of conditions that hold today continue to hold in the future (including, for example, structure of demand and rates of growth), or *if* these conditions change in ways that are specified as part of the forecast, then such and such a future situation will be the result. People who make forecasts do not regard themselves as prophets, nor are they necessarily pleased with the prospects they are forecasting. In essence, they are telling us the probable consequences of present assumptions and present trends; if we do not like the consequences, we can work to change the assumptions and the trends. In this sense, many forecasters would like to be proven wrong. This certainly applies to the ecologists who have forecast worsening environmental problems, and have been mistakenly called prophets of doom while working to avoid it.

Published forecasts of U.S. energy consumption, based on growth rates observed in the early 1960s, range from 1.4 to

1.6 times the 1968 consumption in 1980 and from 2.5 to 3.3 times the 1968 figure in 2000 *(Man's Impact on the Global Environment)*. If the growth rate of the late sixties persists, however, total U.S. energy consumption will increase by 4.7 times between 1968 and 2000. Obviously, forecasts are very sensitive to the growth rate one assumes.

Forecasts for the electrical component of the energy budget as a separate entity are also available. A study prepared for the Joint Economic Committee of the U.S. Congress *(The Economy, Energy, and the Environment)* lists seven such forecasts for 1980 published since 1965, and one published since then for the year 2000. The forecasts for 1980 ranged from 1.8 times to 2.2 times the actual electricity consumption in 1968 (1.43 trillion kwhe). The single forecast for the year 2000 was 4.1 times the 1968 figure. Yet, if the average rate of growth of electrical consumption that actually prevailed between 1965 and 1969 persists, consumption will increase by 2.4 times between 1968 and 1980 and by 9.8 times between 1968 and 2000.

Finally, forecasts for world energy consumption deserve mention. Unfortunately, the data concerning what has happened up until the present are, on the whole, less complete and less reliable than those for the United States, thus making the already difficult art of forecasting even more so. Most observers agree that world energy consumption has been increasing at between 4 and 5 percent per year during the past few decades; forecasts for the next three decades assume rates as high as 5.7 percent per year. The latter figure leads to a doubling time of just over twelve years. Since this is faster growth than even the most sanguine promoter foresees for the United States, it would lead to a gradual reduction of the scandalous fraction of world energy consumption now accounted for by this country.*

---

*Because the population growth rate of the United States is lower than the average for the rest of the world, however, the gap between *per capita* energy consumption here and elsewhere will *widen* as long as U.S. total energy consumption grows within 1 percent as fast as that of the rest of the world.

What is the Energy Crisis?

The essential point about the foregoing forecasts for energy consumption is that they are not predictions and not inevitable. We can insure that they do not come to pass if we decide that the costs outweigh the benefits. The remainder of this part of the book will examine some of those costs and benefits more closely, in terms of the kinds of technologies available to us for the production and conversion of energy, the environmental impact of using those technologies at present and forecasted levels, and the ways in which the energy is likely to be used.

It will become apparent that although practically everyone agrees there is an energy crisis, many people disagree about what it is. The energy industries have tended to regard the forecasts as inevitable and, indeed, desirable. They view the energy crisis as the problem of mobilizing technology and resources quickly enough to achieve the forecasted levels; to them, the growing opposition of environmentalists to their efforts is part of the crisis. (It should be said, though, that the word "crisis" rings hollow coming from utilities that continue to advertise in order to drum up demand.) The environmentalists agree about the existence of a crisis—they see it as the possibility that the forecasted levels of energy consumption might actually be achieved, accompanied by a level of environmental deterioration only hinted at today. And thoughtful observers on both sides worry about the costs of bringing pollution and depletion realistically into the balance sheets, and how the resulting increase in the cost of energy will affect the poor at home and abroad.

This book contains no simple, painless answers—there do not seem to be any. But the following two propositions, at least, seem relevant: first, as economists have known all along, a crisis in supply and demand can be met by moderating demand as well as by increasing supply; second, as biologists have known all along, on this finite planet we must moderate demand eventually. It seems clear that, in terms of energy demand in the United States, the time for moderation is now, and that moderation is possible without returning to a primitive existence or disproportionately burdening the poor.

A Note

Our discussion of energy supply is divided, for convenience, into two categories: how Americans are obtaining energy today, and how we are likely to obtain it in the future. Into the first category go fossil fuels, hydroelectric power, and conventional fission reactors; into the latter go breeder reactors, controlled fusion power, direct harnessing of solar power, and some of the lesser sources such as geothermal, wind, and tidal power.

One should not take this "today-tomorrow" separation too seriously, however, because the distinction is such a fuzzy one. Most of the future sources are already in operation today, albeit on a small scale. Certain developments, such as economic exploitation of the oil shales, could give sources we thought were short-lived a new lease on life. And the distinction between short-term and long-term problems is further blurred by the tremendous inertia that is a built-in characteristic of large-scale energy technologies. For example, a large electric generating station typically has a lifetime of thirty years, but, an additional five to thirteen years are needed to get it from the drawing board into operation in the first place. Thus, decisions we make about alternative power sources today are commitments that determine how *some* of our power will be produced in the year 2000. (Obviously, many decisions between now and then can affect the mix.) We may also find that a rational energy strategy calls for bringing methods we have regarded as long-term into the picture much sooner than that—for example, using solar-powered air conditioners to remove an important potential drain on conventional energy sources during the next twenty years.

2. The Fossil Fuels

Adequacy of supply;
technology and its impact;
air pollution.

The fossil fuels account for about 95 percent of U.S. energy consumption (Figure 1) and 82 percent of our electricity generation. Many people have correctly pointed out that this reliance on fossil fuels is necessarily a passing phenomenon, for we are consuming on a time scale of decades and centuries a resource that accumulated over hundreds of millions of years.

The formation of the fossil fuels can be regarded as a minor detour in the carbon and oxygen cycles of the biosphere. The relevant essentials of the cycles are these: Plants capture incident solar energy and use it to transform carbon dioxide and water into energy-storing carbohydrates, releasing oxygen at the same time. When the plants are eaten and metabolized by decomposers or herbivores, the inverse process occurs—free oxygen is consumed and carbon dioxide, water and energy are released. Throughout the biosphere, these processes balance almost exactly—as much carbon is released and free oxygen consumed in the processes of metabolism as carbon is consumed and oxygen released in the process of photosynthesis. Only a tiny fraction of the carbon in the cycle escapes complete oxidation and is ultimately transformed by further chemical reactions into fossil fuels and their relatives—coal, oil, natural gas liquids, tar and asphalt. Although we can assume that the processes leading to the formation of the fossil fuels are going on today as they have during eons past, the rate is so slow compared to human energy consumption that these fuels are for practical purposes nonrenewable.

Adequacy of Supply

The Analysis of Depletion. The question that first comes to mind in connection with nonrenewable resources is "How soon will they be gone?" The answer for the fossil fuels—and all other resources for that matter—is "never." There will always be some left in the ground. What happens is that we use first the best (most concentrated) supplies and those closest to the surface, until what remains is of such low quality, or so hard to find, or so deep, that it no longer pays to get it out. In the case of energy resources, one can imagine a situation in which it would take more energy to extract a pound of coal or a gallon of oil than could be recovered by burning the fuel once we had it. In practice, the extraction process would become prohibitively uneconomical well before this situation were reached.

As we shall use the terms here, a *resource* refers to how much material is thought to exist; a *reserve* refers to how much is thought to be recoverable under present economic and technological conditions, or, sometimes, to how much is likely to be recoverable under different and specified economic and technological assumptions. Finally, a *proved reserve* is one whose location we already know.

The assessment of reserves is a dynamic business. If the discovery rate exceeds the consumption rate, proved reserves will increase; otherwise they will decrease. Many predictions made in the past about imminent exhaustion of fossil fuels, particularly petroleum, were wrong because they assumed that consumption would increase but reserves would stand still. Slightly better guesses result if one asks how long proved reserves will last at *present* rates of consumption. One knows that both the reserves and the consumption will probably increase, but the assumption is that the two effects will to some extent counterbalance each other.

Among the more sophisticated work on the depletion of fossil fuels is that of geologist M. King Hubbert, of the U.S. Department of the Interior, described in *Resources and Man*. No matter what the resource, says Hubbert, there is a period of increasingly rapid growth in the rate of exploitation as demand increases, the mining industry expands, and costs per unit of material fall. The growth period is followed by a leveling off and then a decline in the rate of consumption, as the resource becomes scarcer and lower in quality more rapidly than can be compensated for by improved technology.

When this rise-and-fall model of consumption applies, the status of a resource can be described by three numbers: the size of the initial supply before any was exploited, the year in which the rate of consumption reaches its peak, and the year when 90 percent of the initial supply is gone. Figure 2 shows estimates of initial supply, peak year, and tailing-off year for some fossil fuel resources. Although our knowledge of the initial supplies may not be terribly accurate, the rise-and-fall pattern is such that errors in the supply estimate do not cause correspondingly large errors in the peak and tailing-off years. For example, even if the discoveries of oil and gas on Alaska's North Slope cause an upward revision of 50 percent in the initial U.S. supplies of these fuels—probably an optimistic estimate—their peak and tailing-off years will be postponed by only a decade.

Various spokesmen have offered wildly differing projections on the subject of fossil fuel depletion, reflecting very different assumptions. To see how this comes about, consider the status of world coal supplies in 1966 from three points of view. The 1966 proved reserves would last 1,440 years at the 1966 rate of consumption. The estimated total initial supply would be 90 percent gone in 122 years if the rate of consumption continued to increase as it had from

1940 to 1966. Finally, the initial supply would be 90 percent gone in 450 years if Hubbert's rise-and-fall pattern prevailed. The last situation is the most realistic of the three. The dramatic differences show that it is easy to be misled.

The apparently very short life expectancy of natural gas supplies, if the calculation is based on proved reserves, has caused much consternation. It has been pointed out that proved reserves of natural gas have, in fact, been decreasing since 1966. Discoveries have not kept pace with consumption. However, the reason for this situation is economic rather than geological. The price of natural gas, which is regulated by the federal government, has been too low to encourage much exploration. To say we are running out of natural gas now (or in ten years) confuses apparent short-term supply with long-term availability.

Nevertheless, it is fair to conclude that under almost any assumptions, the supplies of crude petroleum and natural gas are severely limited. The bulk of the energy likely to flow from these sources may have been tapped within the lifetime of many of the present population. Coal is in much better shape, although even this vast resource cannot absorb the present global rate of increase in consumption (about 3.5 percent per year) for much more than a century. Under more reasonable assumptions, the time horizon for the substantial depletion of proved and probable reserves of coal is at least several centuries.

Tar Sands and Oil Shales. So-called tar sands are saturated with oil too viscous to be recovered by the usual techniques. Owing to this situation, relatively little effort has been spent on locating deposits. However, the tar sands of Alberta alone have been estimated to contain reserves corresponding to more than 500 trillion kwht, or almost twice Hubbert's figure for the initial supply of crude oil in the continental United States. More significantly for the immediate future, some 65 trillion kwht of this amount is thought to be recoverable at a cost competitive with that of crude oil from conventional sources. A commercial plant producing about 50,000 barrels of oil per day (versus a total of 14.7 million

barrels of crude petroleum consumed daily in the United
States) has been in operation since 1967.

Oil shale has an advantage over tar sands in that there
is a greater potential supply, but a disadvantage in that it
is more difficult to exploit. The material is actually an im-
mature form of coal. It must be mined as a solid and then
processed at high temperature to yield the oil, which is significantly different chemically from the crude petroleum/tar
sands family and must undergo further special refining. The
principal U.S. deposits are located in Colorado, Utah and
Wyoming. An amount corresponding to 130 trillion kwht
is thought to be recoverable under present conditions, but
the known resource in North America alone is fifty times
as large. The suspected total resources are staggering: the
equivalent of 500 thousand trillion kwht for North America, and 3 million trillion kwht for the world (*Resources and
Man*). These figures are roughly one hundred times as large as
the initial supply estimates for coal in Figure 2. Many experts believe that most of these oil shales, which range in
quality from 5 to 100 gallons of oil per ton of rock, will
never be exploitable as an energy resource. (Hubbert believes they have more promise as a source of raw material
for petrochemicals and plastics.) However, "never" is a
stronger word than past experience predicting the course of
technology seems to justify.

Presumably, the technology of exploiting both tar sands
and oil shales would have been pushed more vigorously than
it has if continued discoveries in the Middle East, in the
South Pacific, and on our own continental shelves had not
seemed to assure an adequate supply of petroleum in conventional form. A "semi-works" oil shale operation—larger
than pilot size but smaller than commercial—is now underway in western Colorado. One suspects that increases in the
cost of energy from other sources may lead to the rapid
expansion of such enterprises. It also seems likely that in-
tensive exploitation and research might lead to an upward
revision in the fraction of this vast resource thought to be
recoverable.

Gasification and Liquefaction of Coal. Tar sands and oil shales are not the only recourse as conventional supplies of petroleum and natural gas dwindle. The technology to convert part of our considerable reserves of coal to liquid and gaseous fuels already exists, and is moving to make these processes cheaper as conventional fuels promise to become more expensive. Gasification of coal is farthest along. In Europe, where natural gas is more expensive than in the United States, gas has been obtained from coal on a commercial scale for many years. The most efficient plants now in operation produce gas from coal at a cost of about $3.40 per 1,000 kwht, which is two to three times the cost paid for natural gas by most consumers in the United States. Nevertheless, most experts believe that rising prices for natural gas and improvements in coal gasification will make the latter competitive here by the late 1970s.

Liquefaction of coal has also been technologically feasible for a long time; the Germans did it in World War II, when cost was no object. Landsberg and Schurr *(Energy in the United States)* quote current estimates of nine to thirteen cents per gallon of gasoline produced from coal, which is approaching competitiveness with gasoline refined from crude petroleum. Evidently the liquefaction of coal is ready to serve if future scarcity should drive up the price of oil.

In view of the established potential of coal for alleviating forecasted shortages in the more portable fossil fuels, one wonders why the federal government has spent so little research and development money to assure that technology and sheer capacity could be brought to bear if needed. One estimate put government expenditures for energy research in the mid-1960s at almost 70 percent for nuclear energy, 10 percent for gas and oil, and no more than 4 percent for any other source, including coal. This seems a curious set of priorities because nuclear generated electricity can replace neither oil nor gas until massive, time-consuming changes have been accomplished in industrial and transportation technologies.

Imports. Another aspect of the supply question is the extent to which the United States depends on foreign sources to meet energy demand. Today we import 23 percent of the liquid fossil fuels we consume,* and some observers believe this could rise to 40 percent by 1980. On the other hand, the United States exports more coal than any other country in the world, almost all of it going to Japan, Canada and Europe. These exports of coal total about one-quarter the amount of energy imported in the form of gas and oil.

The present situation exists not because of any theoretical inability of domestic reserves to meet requirements in the short term but because foreign crude oil and residual fuel oil, which make up the bulk of the imports, are cheaper than that from domestic sources. Practically speaking, sudden discontinuation of the flow of foreign oil would cause shortages because the U.S. oil industry is not mobilized to meet the total demand. If it were not for quotas imposed by the federal government on the importation of crude oil, the price differential would lead to still larger use of foreign oil.

The extent of our reliance on imports and the wisdom of the quota system which seeks to limit it are the subject of continuing controversy. One side holds that national security is threatened by dependence on energy sources that could be cut off by hostilities or made more expensive at the whim of the producers. The opposition argues that we should take advantage of foreign oil while it's cheap, so that ours will still be there when things get tight. Another point often made is that removing the protective system of quotas would force the U.S. oil industry to abandon some of its antiquated and inefficient practices.

There is a more serious dilemma in the import situation, which is common to many resources besides oil. Exporting countries, mostly underdeveloped and—except for their oil —poor, desperately want our money. But it may not be in their long-term interests or those of their fellows in other

*The widely held belief that most U.S. imports of petroleum come from the Middle East is erroneous. The major sources of imports in 1968 were: 60 percent from Central and South America, 20 percent from Canada and Mexico, and only 8 percent from the Middle East.

underdeveloped countries to be selling us today the cheapest reserves of high-grade energy in the world. We could afford now to exploit domestic reserves at a higher cost, and we will be able to do so in the future. But the underdeveloped countries themselves may find, as their energy needs grow and their fiscal means stay relatively meager, that they have sold for a fast dollar their own passport to some semblance of development.

Some Conclusions. All told, the future of fossil fuel supplies is not as constricted as some people (particularly the proponents of a fast switch to a fission energy economy) have been telling us. The time horizon for conventional liquid and gaseous fossil fuels does seem short—possibly only fifty years until the bulk of the exploitable resource is gone. But the options for replacing these fuels with oil and gas derived from coal, tar sands and oil shales have not yet been vigorously pursued, mainly because there has been little incentive to do so. The existence of such staggering quantities of *potential* fossil fuel as the oil shales makes it at least possible that absolute supply would not limit human energy use for centuries, even without nuclear fuels or direct harnessing of solar energy.

We should ask, of course, whether it is wise to burn as fuel and thus destroy forever resources as versatile as our coal, oil and gas. Their complex hydrocarbon molecules are useful as the basis of lubricants, plastics and a vast array of other petrochemicals. Fortunately, hydrocarbons used in many of these ways are, at least in principle, recyclable. Crankcase oil from automobiles can be cleaned and used again, and ways will surely be found to recycle many kinds of plastics. Recycling should operate to stabilize a demand that today, without significant recycling, is only a small fraction of the total for coal, gas and oil.* Finally, it seems likely that we will be able to pay more for raw materials that can be

---

*Despite the fact that use of plastics in the United States now exceeds in volume the combined use of aluminum and copper, the petrochemical industry supplying these plastics uses less than 2 percent of all fossil fuels consumed.

reused many times than for a source of energy that can be used only once. This will mean that fossil fuel resources of quality too low to be profitably extracted and processed for energy production can be tapped for other uses, as Hubbert has suggested for the oil shales.

None of the foregoing is to suggest, however, that the United States can safely persist with present trends in the use of fossil fuels—even if we continue with our traditional attitude of "the poor countries be damned." The pressing reason we must slow down is, again, not that we are running out of fuel but rather that the environmental costs of getting it, moving it and burning it are reaching unacceptable levels.

Technology and Its Impact

The production of energy from fossil fuels involves actual or potential adverse impact on man and his environment at a number of stages: exploration; the extraction, processing, and transportation of the fuel; and consumption itself. In the case of electricity, conversion and transmission must be added to the list between transportation of fuel and consumption.

Exploration. The environmental consequences of exploring for new reserves of fossil fuels are relatively minor. They include taking roads and equipment into wilderness areas (probably most serious in the case of searching for oil in the fragile subarctic regions); the use of explosives, particularly underwater, to help determine the oil-bearing potential of the underlying geological strata; and the visual pollution associated with test wells.

Extraction and Processing. The disruptions of exploration are dwarfed by those caused by the extractive activities following a successful search. In the case of oil and gas, problems include the visual impact of drilling rigs dispersed over vast areas, and the disposal of three barrels of salty brine produced, on the average, along with every barrel of oil.*

---

*Most oil occurs in combination with underground reservoirs of salt water, which cannot be prevented from coming up the well along with the oil.

Considerably more serious are the ecological costs of blowouts. These initial eruptions of gas, water and oil under
pressure are less frequent than they once were. It is in the
economic interest of the oil producers to prevent them.
Those that occur on dry land are usually easily controlled
and affect only a limited area, although the consequences may
be particularly severe in the far north. Those that occur offshore are more difficult to control, as we have discovered
off Santa Barbara and Louisiana; the spread of the oil over
large areas of ocean seems the inevitable result. Oil from
such blowouts and from routine seepage and spillage in offshore operations accounts for an estimated 10 percent of the
2.3 million tons of oil man adds to the world's oceans each
year *(Man's Impact on the Global Environment)*.

Unfortunately, this extraction-related contribution takes
place in the shallow continental shelf areas where biological
productivity is highest. The refining of crude petroleum into
gasoline, kerosene, fuel oils and so forth results in additional
discharges to the oceans—an estimated 15 percent of the
2.3 million tons. Obvious consequences of all this oil are the
degradation of the coastal environment for human use, and
the local poisoning of marine life. Young animals are affected
especially severely because the bays and estuaries where
many spills occur serve as the nurseries for much sea life.
Oil may also cause more far-reaching effects, yet to be understood, in the major ocean food chains that man depends
upon for an important part of his protein. A recent study
prepared for the Joint Economic Committee of the U.S. Congress deemed the entire problem sufficiently severe to advo-
cate a "go slower" policy in offshore drilling.

The extraction of coal also imposes serious environmental
costs, some of them obvious to anyone who drives through
the sections of Pennsylvania, Ohio, West Virginia, Kentucky
and other states that have been ravaged by strip mining. In
recent years, strip mining has accounted for about one-third
of U.S. coal production; the fraction is expected to increase.
This method uses massive steam shovels and other earth-
moving equipment to strip the overburden of rock and soil

from shallow-lying coal seams. The surface material is piled to one side while the coal is scooped out, a process executed for the length of the seam. The resulting mountains of discarded overburden not only constitute a visual disaster where they stand but also often migrate downhill and downstream to scar valleys, clog streams and kill fish. Rainfall leaches toxic substances from the newly exposed material, creating a serious water pollution problem.

It is argued by the coal industry that stripped land can be reclaimed for some uses at a cost ranging from $200 to $800 per acre. The higher figure amounts to only about 2 percent of the market price of the coal extracted, yet the better part of the 1.3 million acres affected by U.S. strip mining for coal until 1965 had nevertheless not been reclaimed. It should be noted also that farmland that has been stripped can generally not be restored to productivity at any price, nor is reclamation feasible in steep terrain.

Underground mining supplies the other two-thirds of U.S. coal production. Perhaps the most serious problem here is the poor working conditions in the mines, which tend to be hot, damp, foul of atmosphere and laden with the coal dust implicated in the miners' dreaded "black lung" disease. Cave-ins and gas explosions are additional liabilities. Not surprisingly, a shortage of coal miners is anticipated if the use of coal in electric generation undergoes the expected increase in the coming decades. One result of such a shortage may be an even faster increase in strip mining, which depends more heavily on machinery than on labor.

There is little to cheer about in either form of mining. The piles of wastes from underground mines create acid drainage problems and other hazards similar to those mentioned above in connection with strip mining. Subsidence of the surface above underground mines is common, as are long-burning underground fires. Finally, some 60 percent of the coal mined in this country is washed, creating an additional water pollution problem and producing 90 million tons of solid waste annually.

The future mining of oil shales will pose special problems

in waste disposal. The solid residue remaining after the shale has been brought to the surface and the oil extracted amounts to 80 percent or more of the original weight of the material. A moderate-sized commercial operation producing enough oil from high-grade shale to run one large electric power plant (say, 1 million kwe) would produce some 15 million tons of waste annually. The president of Atlantic Richfield, which is a participant in the existing protoype oil shale operation, has an enlightened solution in store. He said in a recent interview: "Some of [the spent shale] can be used to fill up a few of the canyons and valleys of the rather desolate parts of Utah, Colorado, and Wyoming in which oil shale is found."*

Transportation. The expense of transporting fossil fuels can comprise a considerable part of its ultimate cost. Fuel-transportation considerations are often important in determining the locations of industrial plants and electric generating stations. At one time the average cost of transporting coal to its destination exceeded the value of the coal at the mine; transportation costs averaged 70 percent of the value at the mine in the late 1960s. Proximity to large deposits of cheap, strippable coal is one reason for the location of a new generation of massive power plants in the American Southwest (see page 161).

The unit train method of transporting coal is a relatively recent development. Such trains consist solely of coal cars and typically operate on a single, fixed route—full from mine to power plant or steel mill and empty back again. We will be seeing more of them, but their environmental drawbacks—noise and spillage of coal from open cars—are relatively minor. Closed cars are proposed to remedy the second problem in the future.

As one might expect, the cheapest means of transporting fossil fuels—oil pipelines and tankers—pose the greatest hazards. In both cases, the problem is spillage. For overland pipelines this threat is particularly serious where the local

---

*U.S. News and World Report, May 10, 1971.

biological communities are relatively fragile or where there
are many rivers. Both conditions hold true for the proposed
trans-Alaska pipeline. Spillage of oil from tankers, on the
other hand, is not merely the result of the occasional, well-
publicized mishap. It is also the routine consequence of
everyday operations, including transfers at docks and between vessels, and cleaning of tanks. These "normal" operations account for an estimated 25 percent of man's total discharge of oil to the oceans; accidental spills account for 5
percent. The biological and human consequences of oil in
the oceans were mentioned above. As with many environmental problems, the full extent of past and potential damage is unknown. This lack of knowledge is hardly reassuring.
DDT and mercury have already demonstrated that ignorance
is not bliss.

Definitive answers about the effect of oil in the oceans
may come with increases in the input. About 60 percent of
the world's production of oil is moved by sea. The discovery
that shipping costs per barrel decrease rapidly as the size of
the tanker increases has generated a trend toward larger and
larger vessels. The *Torrey Canyon,* at 117,000 deadweight
tons, was considered a large tanker when she went aground
off England in 1967 and gave up her oil to the sea. Today
vessels four times as large are under construction; the loss
of one of these, fully loaded, could in one stroke increase
man's annual discharge of oil to the oceans by 20 percent.

Consumption and Conversion. The best-known environmental consequences associated with the fossil fuels occur
when the coal, gas or oil is burned. As we have already seen,
this occurs in a variety of places: the engines of trains, trucks,
automobiles and aircraft; the burners of household and commercial ranges and heating systems; the blast furnaces of the
steel industry; the boilers that make the steam that drives the
turbines that generate electricity.

If our only fossil fuels were hydrocarbons, free of impurities, and if they could be burned completely and in oxygen
rather than in air, the sole products of combustion would
be carbon dioxide (CO_2), water vapor (H_2O) and heat—

which are not always innocuous. But, because the "ifs" are not true, many more immediately dangerous substances result. The burning of sulfur and various other mineral impurities in fossil fuels produces ash and very toxic oxides of sulfur. Burning is rarely complete, particularly in internal combustion engines, which operate as a series of explosions rather than as a steady flame. Thus carbon monoxide (CO) and unburned hydrocarbons result. And because most combustion occurs in an atmosphere that is 78 percent nitrogen, when the temperature is high enough nitrogen oxides are produced.

Figure 3 shows the origin of the five principal classes of air pollutants for the United States during 1968. Obviously, the burning of fossil fuels is not the only source of air pollution but it is the most important one. Additionally, the fossil fuels make important contributions to air pollution at stages other than consumption: oil refining and the production of coke from coal are included in the "industrial processes" category in Figure 3, and emissions from coal waste fires and gasoline marketing are included under "miscellaneous."

Mounting evidence connects levels of air pollution with various adverse effects on human health. The oxides of sulfur* are considered the most dangerous of the air pollutants listed. They are implicated in rising death rates from bronchitis, emphysema, lung cancer, and other respiratory ailments. Adverse effects on health are thought to be possible at sulfur dioxide (SO_2) concentrations as low as .04 parts per million. Carbon monoxide, by comparison, begins to have detectable effects only at 10 to 30 parts per million. The oxides of sulfur have the particularly insidious property of interacting *synergistically* with particulate matter: the combined effect of the two contaminants when both are present exceeds the sum of the effects that would be experienced if they acted independently.

---

*Oxides of sulfur include both the sulfur dioxide (SO_2) which constitutes the bulk of the emissions, and the sulfur trioxide (SO_3) that is formed from SO_2 by oxidation.

Certain hydrocarbons are cancer-causing agents, but the level of concentration in air in which they become so is unknown. Other hydrocarbons react with the oxides of nitrogen* to form photochemical smog, which includes ozone and other oxidants. These substances cause eye irritation, aggravate respiratory ailments such as asthma, and impair physical performance even in healthy individuals. Oxides of nitrogen, in addition to participating in the production of photochemical smog, interfere directly with respiratory function and may increase susceptibility to disease. Carbon monoxide in concentrations common in today's cities slows reactions (increasing the probability of accidents) and probably places an additional burden on individuals suffering from anemia and diseases of the heart and lungs.

Particulate matter at levels typical in urban areas has been associated, in one study, with a rise in the overall death rate, and, in others, with certain kinds of cancer. Specific kinds of particulate matter, such as asbestos from construction materials and brake linings, and lead deliberately added to gasoline, are known health hazards at high concentrations. They may well be dangerous at the lower levels encountered routinely in cities. Mercury, a serious environmental problem in its own right, is a contaminant in coal and oil; it is possible that burning these fuels may exceed all other man-made sources of environmental mercury combined. The ash produced when coal is burned contains small quantities of radioactive radium and thorium. There has been some controversy over whether the resulting release of radioactivity from coal-burning power plants is more serious than that from nuclear reactors, but the most comprehensive study published to date concludes that it is not.**

*Only two of the eight oxides of nitrogen are important pollutants—nitric oxide (NO), which is formed in large amounts when combustion takes place in air at high temperature, and nitrogen dioxide, which is formed by the oxidation of NO once the latter is emitted.

**The study, performed by the U.S. Public Health Service, appears in the Hearings on Environmental Effects of Producing Electric Power, Part I, Joint Committee on Atomic Energy, 1969.

The complexity of the effects of air pollution and the incompleteness of present knowledge mean that one cannot simply take the figures in Figure 3 as valid indicators of responsibility for the problem. Automobiles alone contributed 39 percent of U.S. air pollution *by weight* in 1968, but much of this was carbon monoxide, one of the least dangerous pollutants. A more reasonable measure of who is doing what to whom is obtained by multiplying the weight of the emissions from each source by an estimate of the relative hazard of the pollutants involved. It is impossible to get precise agreement on such toxicity estimates, but use of any reasonable figures leads to the conclusion that emissions from fossil fueled electric power plants are a bigger component of the total hazard than simple weight considerations show. This is so because most of the oxides of sulfur come from such plants, and they are considerably more toxic on a pound-for-pound basis than the carbon monoxide so prominent in automotive emissions.

In addition to its effect on health, air pollution can damage crops, shrubs, and trees; corrode metal structures and erode stone ones; acidify natural bodies of water and reduce the fertility of soil; damage and discolor fabrics; and, of course, impair visibility. Allowing for these damages and those to health, the President's Council on Environmental Quality estimates that the economic costs of air pollution in in our country is "many billions of dollars." If it should be, say, $10 billion in all, with two-thirds attributable in one way or another to energy consumption, this hidden cost would equal almost 25 percent of the part of GNP generated by the energy industries in 1969.

Various strategies for control of the air pollution problem are possible; a comprehensive study by the American Chemical Society *(Cleaning Our Environment: The Chemical Basis for Action)* identified five basic options:

(1) Use fuels that do not contain the pollutants or the substances that become pollutants.

(2) Remove the pollutants or pre-pollutants from the fuel.

(3) Burn the fuel in a way that minimizes generation of the pollutants.

(4) Remove the pollutants from the combustion products.

(5) Replace the process with one that does not generate the pollutants.

A strategy conspicuous by its absence here and in most similar lists—burn less fuel—will be considered later.

The advantages and drawbacks of the five strategies can be seen by considering attempts to control automotive air pollution. Use of low-lead or no-lead fuel is an example of strategy (1). A major disadvantage is that the substitute may be as bad or worse (certain complex hydrocarbons, possibly cancer causers, in exchange for lead). A second drawback is that much of the pollution is caused by basic constituents of the fuel, which also rules out strategy (2). Most automotive pollution control employs strategy (3): fuel-air ratio, timing and other factors are adjusted to foster complete combustion, minimizing CO and hydrocarbon emissions. Additionally, pollutant-containing gases escaping past the cylinder rings are recycled to the engine inlet. A disadvantage is that different pollutants may require conflicting measures— some adjustments that limit CO and hydrocarbons foster the formation of nitrogen oxides. Control of nitrogen oxides will probably ultimately require the use of strategy (4) in the form of catalytic reactors. A sufficient description of these for our purposes is that they are complicated, expensive and quickly rendered ineffective if the fuel contains lead. Finally, to the extent that even CO_2 and water vapor are pollutants, strategy (4) cannot succeed—it is infeasible to collect and store all exhaust gases.

The liabilities of the first four strategies as they apply to automobiles are easily summarized: some shift the impact rather than removing it, all become more difficult and more expensive as the required degree of control increases, and all of them together leave some pollutants untouched. Meeting the 1975 federal standards may cost $300 per automobile. By 1985 the sheer number of cars projected will cause total emissions of carbon monoxide to begin to rise again. Strategy (5), replacing the process, is more radical than the others but is no panacea either. E.g., replacing the internal combustion engine with a steam engine would reduce emissions but not to zero. Switching to electric automobiles, if their many technical problems could be solved, would shift the environmental burden from the vicinity of highways to the vicinity of power plants. It has been argued that pollution is more easily controlled at a few hundred power plants than at several million individual internal combustion engines. As we shall see, it may be easier, but it is not easy and it is not cheap.

To understand the pollution problem at electric power plants, we must briefly examine the technology of the energy conversion process. Fuel (coal, oil or gas) is burned in the boiler; water flowing in tubes in the boiler walls is thereby converted to high pressure steam. This steam drives a turbine, which turns the generator which produces the electricity. Energy still left in the steam when it leaves the turbine is transferred to a coolant when the steam is changed back to water in the condenser. The water then enters the boiler to repeat the process.

The toll exacted by the second law of thermodynamics (see Chapter 1) is paid mainly at the stack and at the condenser, where the greater part of the energy originally stored in the fuel is carried uselessly away by warm combustion products or warm river water. The thermal efficiency of the plant tells us how much waste heat there is for a given output of electrical energy—the higher the efficiency, the less waste heat. A modern fossil fuel plant may have an efficiency of 40 percent. The average efficiency of all U.S. plants is about 32 percent. Because the environmental impact of waste heat and the technology for ameliorating it are associated with nuclear as well as fossil fuel plants, these subjects will be treated in a separate section.

In an hour's operation, a 1 million kwe, 40 percent efficient coal plant burns 340 tons of coal and produces 940 tons of carbon dioxide, 17 tons of sulfur dioxide, 3.4 tons of oxides of nitrogen, and 34 tons of ash. Even if most of the ash is prevented from escaping out of the stack, the 800 tons of it produced daily in our sample plant pose a considerable waste disposal problem. Ash can be used in cement and other construction materials, but this is not done much in the United States because other raw materials for construction are cheaper. Instead, the customary method of "disposing" of it has been to pile it on the ground in the vicinity of the power plant. The estimated 200 million tons of ash so deposited during the last ten years has resulted in dry ash blowing about, causing air pollution and water pollution. Additionally, rain water leaches chemicals from the piles, causing crop destruction, and the piles themselves are an eyesore.

The pollution from a plant burning high-sulfur fuel oil is about the same as from a coal-burning plant of the same efficiency, except that less particulate matter is produced. Natural gas, by comparison, is a standout—it produces several thousand times less sulfur dioxide per kwhe, and on the average about half as much of the oxides of nitrogen.

To provide a reference point for our discussion of the technology and cost of pollution control for fossil fuel electric power plants, it is helpful to know the expense of building and operating them without special pollution control measures. Construction costs are particularly hard to pin down because they have been rising rapidly as the price of labor increases. A reasonable figure for a large coal plant with no thermal pollution control measures and only the height of its exhaust stacks to alleviate air pollution is about $135 per kwe of capacity. This means that a plant capable of generating 1 million kwe would cost $135 million to build. When translated through the intricacies of financing and writing off the cost of the plant during a twenty- or thirty-year period of operation, this comes to about 3/10 of a

cent (three mills) per kwhe of electricity actually generated.*
Operating costs and maintenance, not including fuel cost,
amount to another 1/10 of a cent per kwhe, and the fuel
adds, on the average, a bit over 2/10 of a cent. Thus the
total cost of producing electric power in a modern coal-fired
plant with no special investment in pollution control is
roughly 6/10 of a cent or six mills per kwhe. To this amount
there is added an average of about eight mills per kwhe in
transmission and distribution costs. Thus, the cost of producing electricity and getting it to the consumer is about 1.5
cents per kwhe. In practice, large commercial and industrial
users of electricity pay this amount or less, while residential users pay more—typically 2.0 to 2.5 cents per kwhe.

Now let's consider again the possible strategies for the
control of air pollution—how they apply to fossil fuel electric power plants, what their drawbacks are in this context, and how much they may increase the cost of power.
Strategy (1) may take several forms: use coal or fuel oil
that does not contain much sulfur, or switch to gas. Unfortunately, only a fifth of U. S. coal contains less than 1 percent sulfur, and the low-sulfur deposits are mainly in the
West. The premium for this coal on the eastern market,
where it is in great demand to meet stringent regulations,
amounts to as much as 50 percent above the usual price of
coal. Moreover, even 1 percent sulfur is too much—New
Jersey now requires 0.2 percent sulfur content or less, or
other measures must be taken to reduce emissions to correspond to those for low-sulfur coal. Low-sulfur fuel oil is also
scarce and costly. Any large-scale switch to gas would probably require gasifying coal to produce it. This would double

---

*This calculation requires estimating the *load factor* of the plant during
its operating lifetime. The load factor is the amount of electricity actually
generated divided by the amount that *could* be generated. It is always less
than 100 percent because demand varies from hour to hour, day to day,
and season to season, while the plant (or network of plants) must be designed to meet the peak demand. The average load factor for all capacity
in the United States, fossil fuel and otherwise, was only a little more than
50 percent in 1969. New plants, being more efficient, get the heaviest use,
and load factors of 70 percent are common.

fuel costs if it were done at the 1970 price of gasification, but the cost penalty will decrease during the next several years. This is probably the most promising approach within strategy (1) because, unlike the others, it considerably reduces particulate and nitrogen oxide emissions as well as those of SO_2. The major drawback may be the long delay necessary to construct large gasification plants and put them into operation.

Strategy (2), removal of the pollutant from the fuel, is expensive and imperfect. The usual processes remove only inorganic sulfur from coal, leaving the organic forms—an average of half the amount originally present—untouched. Only gasification removes it all. The sulfur content of fuel oil can be reduced from 2.0 percent to 0.5 percent for a 50 percent increase in the price of the fuel. Further reductions in sulfur content become disproportionately expensive. An additional drawback of low-sulfur fuel, natural or desulfurized, is that some boilers cannot handle it without expensive modifications.

Strategy (3), modification of the combustion process, is incorporated in special furnace design to reduce nitrogen oxide emissions by as much as 40 to 50 percent. Beyond this, however, there is virtually no technology in prospect for nitrogen oxide abatement in power plants.

Strategy (4) has long been practiced in the form of various devices to scour the particulate matter from combustion gases. The most widely used of these is the electrostatic precipitator: the latest models remove 98 percent or more of the fly ash from stack gases. Typical initial cost for such a device is about $5 per kwe of plant capacity. One shortcoming is that uncollected particles tend to be the smallest ones, i.e. those suspected of the most severe health effects. Another is that some electrostatic precipitators are ineffective (as low as 50 percent removal) when low-sulfur coal is used.

Technology for the removal of sulfur dioxide from stack gases has been under investigation for thirty years. Several processes are thought to be promising, but none is operating in a full scale power plant. The cheapest and most adaptable one for use in existing plants unfortunately doubles the amount of solid waste material generated per kwhe. Initial investment for this method will be perhaps $10 per kwe of plant capacity; operating costs will be equivalent to a 25 percent increase in the cost of the fuel. The alternative processes will cost perhaps $30 per kwe of capacity and may increase the operating cost of fuel by 75 percent. But they will produce saleable sulfur or sulfuric acid, which could defray the operating expense if a market for these commodities exists. The amount of sulfur dioxide removed by all these processes is expected to be between 90 and 95 percent of that produced.

Unfortunately, neither the cost nor the effectiveness of the technologies for removing sulfur dioxide will be proven until full-scale devices are built. At $10 per kwe, this means a $10-million experiment to test a unit for a one million kilowatt plant. People who argue that power station pollution control should be easy compared to control of millions of automobiles are correct insofar as inspection, maintenance, and enforcement are concerned. But the prohibitive cost of doing experiments on the required scale means that control technology for power plants will be much slower to be developed than that for cars.

An alternative to "tacked-on" pollution-control systems is complete redesign of the combustion stage of coal-fueled power generation. Proponents of one design* argue that it would control particulates and sulfur, and simultaneously decrease construction costs. They claim that coal research in this country has been stifled by lack of funds, and that a reasonable reallocation of priorities in energy research would lead to coal plants superior in every respect to today's plants. They are probably right. The principal practical drawback may (again) be the time required for new designs to be developed, proved, and to constitute a major proportion of the plants in operation.

---

*This design is the so-called *fluidized-bed* high pressure boiler. The reader interested in details should consult the article by chemical engineer Arthur M. Squires in *Science* magazine, August 28, 1970.

So far we have discussed only the first four strategies for pollution control. The fifth is the one advocated by proponents of nuclear power—replace the process with a non-polluting one. Unfortunately, this solution has pollutants and hazards of its own. For completeness, we should mention another strategy that has played a part in bringing massive coal power plants to remote parts of the Southwest (see page 161): move the polluters away from the people. This approach, by which the citizens of Los Angeles and Phoenix dump the environmental burden of their consumption on a helpless minority of Navajos hundreds of miles away, has the advantage of minimizing the number of individuals and amount of property harmed by the pollution. It has the disadvantages of being morally bankrupt and irretrievably destructive to wilderness.

Transmission. The transmission of electric power from power plant to distribution point is not without environmental drawbacks. Such lines are becoming more noticeable with the trend toward large power stations located outside the urban areas served. Another factor causing proliferation of transmission lines is the increasing use of interties connecting many utilities into large power grids, which increase load factors by using otherwise idle capacity in one region to meet peak demand in another. The grids are also supposed to provide back-up capacity against local equipment failures, although the northeastern power grid did not function quite this way in the blackout of 1965.

The cost of transmission at present amounts to an average of 10 percent of the total cost of electricity generated from coal. Distribution from substation to the individual user accounts for another 40 percent. The capacity of transmission lines increases very rapidly (and the cost per kwhe of energy moved decreases) as the operating voltage is increased.* Thus the trend has been toward higher and higher voltages as the technology becomes available.

---

*One kwhe can be moved 400 miles on a 550-thousand-volt line for about 2/10 of a cent; the same money buys only 200 miles on a 220-thousand-volt line.

Unfortunately, higher voltages aggravate both major environmental costs of transmission systems: the visual intrusion of the towers and cables becomes greater because of increased size, and more land is taken up because high voltage lines require a wider right-of-way (200 feet or more for a single line). Already in 1970, some four million acres of U.S. land—an area larger than the state of Connecticut—were occupied by transmission lines. One possible solution is to put the lines underground. But this is expensive, and various technical difficulties must be overcome before it can be done for high-voltage lines. A more immediate solution is to make transmission rights-of-way available for recreational or other uses. Some attempts have been made to design more attractive towers and less conspicuous cables.

3. Hydroelectric Energy

Hydroelectric energy is electricity produced from the energy of falling water. This is actually stored solar energy: the water being lifted from the sea and carried to high elevations in the course of the hydrological cycle, which is driven by the sun. Hydroelectric energy has several striking advantages over other current ways of producing electricity. No fuel is required, since the energy comes from the sun. There are no combustion products, no other wastes from the generation process, and there is almost no localized thermal pollution—only heat loss from friction in the turbines and generators, and electrical losses in transmission and distribution. Even the heat that eventually results from using the electricity is not an added burden on the environment because an equivalent amount of heat would have been produced by friction if the water had been allowed to fall undisturbed and unharnessed. Finally, hydroelectric energy is cheap—as long as it does not have to be transmitted too far to reach its users.

The liabilities to be weighed against these assets are that usable hydroelectric sites are in limited supply, that there are ecological and esthetic costs associated with exploiting these sites, and that the eventual filling of reservoirs with silt destroys their usefulness. The first problem does not mean there is a limited amount of hydroelectric energy (the supply will last as long as the sun and the oceans do) but that there are only so many sites at which this continuously renewed energy source can be economically tapped.

The capacity of hydroelectric installations in this country at the end of 1969 was 53 million kwe, and these facilities produced 17 percent of the electricity consumed here. Thus hydroelectric energy accounted for only about 4 percent of the total U.S. energy use.* Although the production of electricity at hydroelectric plants has been increasing steadily, its fraction of the electricity budget has been falling because other sources have been growing more rapidly. The Federal Power Commission believes, based on stream flow records and surveys of feasible dam sites, that about 125 million kwe of potential capacity remains to be developed, mostly in the Pacific Northwest and in Alaska. Unless present trends change drastically, the fraction of electricity produced by hydroelectric plants will continue to drop even if the additional potential capacity is used.

Harnessing hydroelectric energy is usually just a matter of building a dam with turbines and generators installed at the base. The energy that would have been dissipated as the water descended over the submerged steam bed is then stored as potential energy in the form of water held up behind the dam. When electricity is needed, tunnels through the dam are opened so that stored energy—the high pressure of a column of water tens or hundreds of feet high— drives water through them with great force, spinning turbines

---

*This figure varies with the method of accounting. Most books compute hydro's role in the total energy budget as based on how much fuel would have to be burned at 33 percent efficiency to generate the same amount of electricity. This leads to the 4 percent figure used here. However, because hydroelectric stations are almost 100 percent efficient, the actual amount of energy involved is only one-third of this. The fraction of all electricity generated is still 17 percent, but the fraction of total energy use is only about 1.3 percent.

which turn generators much like those in steam plants. Some hydroelectric installations have capacities equal to the largest fossil fuel and nuclear plants: there are five plants of more than 700,000 kwe on the Columbia River, and one of 2 million kwe on the Niagara.

In practice, hydroelectric energy has been much less expensive than other types. The price of electricity delivered to consumers in the Northwest, where hydroelectric units comprise more than 90 percent of all installed electric capacity, has averaged less than half the cost in other parts of the country. On the other hand, it is difficult to say what hydroelectric power would cost if it reflected the full price of the dam projects. Because such projects are often judged to have other benefits besides power production, especially flood control and water supply, the recipients of these benefits foot some of the bill. Additionally, a great deal of federal money is usually involved.

The esthetic objection to hydroelectric projects is that they turn some of the nation's most beautiful gorges and river valleys into large, dull lakes. For those who enjoy power-boating, water-skiing, and warm-water fishing, this may be considered a benefit. Probably the most powerful conservation argument on this point is that there are already a great many lakes where such activities can be pursued, but very few remaining gorges and wild rivers. In some instances, hydroelectric projects cover prime farmland, which eventually proves to be a poor trade. For those whose homes and livelihoods have been submerged, the personal cost of hydroelectric power is high.

Hydroelectric dams and their reservoirs may have other adverse effects, as well. The spawning grounds of migratory fishes of commercial and recreational importance, such as salmon, are often destroyed, or the fish are prevented from reaching them. The proposed Rampart Dam in Alaska would have destroyed one of the great remaining wildlife habitats on the North American continent. Seepage from reservoirs may raise the water table and bring subsurface salts and minerals with it, impairing the fertility of the soil. Reservoirs lose water by evaporation in proportion to their surface area (and depending also on local climatic conditions), increasing the concentration of dissolved minerals in the water remaining. And, in some instances, the filling of large reservoirs has triggered earthquakes because the weight of the water accumulating shifted the balance of stresses on the earth's crust.

Finally, hydroelectric reservoirs are subject to eventual filling with the silt that is carried in varying quantities by every river. Rivers such as the Colorado, which carries a particularly heavy burden of silt, may succeed in filling large reservoirs after one or two centuries. In other rivers, the process may take longer but can be accelerated by erosion from logging or upstream development. Whatever the case, the storage capacity of the reservoir is eventually destroyed. When that happens, one can still tap the energy of the waterfall that then occupies the dam site, but the available energy is then completely subject to the fluctuations in river flow.

Another process utilizing the energy of falling water is called *pumped storage*. This involves two reservoirs, a high one and a low one, connected by pipes containing dual-purpose pump-turbines. During periods of low demand, such as late at night, electricity pumps water from the lower reservoir to the higher one. Later, when demand is high, the water is allowed to fall back to the lower reservoir, spinning the turbines and generating electricity. Because it takes about 30 percent more power to pump the water uphill than is recovered when it comes back down, pumped storage power makes sense only as a means of meeting peak demand. The utilities can afford it because the pumping is done when their "base-load" plants would otherwise be idle. The extra cost of running them is only the cost of the fuel—perhaps 2/10's of a cent per kwhe. When the electricity is recovered later to meet actual needs in the power grid, it can be sold for three times as much.

Most environmental disruption caused by a pumped storage facility results from the upper reservoir (the lower one is usually an already existing lake or stream). The disruption usually is less than that at most hydroelectric sites because the upper storage reservoir can be relatively small. On the other hand, the visual problem may be aggravated because the water level fluctuates wildly according to how much energy is being stored. This exposes large expanses of ugly mud and discourages recreational use.

4. Nuclear Fission

Adequacy of fuel supply;
radiation and public health; technological
impact; economics and subsidies;
regulation and conflict of interest.

Nuclear fission was the source of energy for almost exactly 1 percent of the electricity generated in the United States during 1969. Since generation of electricity is the only way in which we are harnessing fission energy today, and since the production of electricity accounts for less than a fourth of total energy use in the United States, the contribution of fission to the energy budget as a whole in 1969 was less than one-quarter of 1 percent.

The amount of installed nuclear generating capacity and the amount of electricity actually generated by these plants, however, has been doubling approximately every two years since 1961. The Atomic Energy Commission (AEC) believes that this very rapid growth will continue, so that half of all electricity generated in the year 2000 will be from nuclear plants. Most projections claim that by then electricity from all sources will total 40 to 50 percent of total U.S. energy consumption. Acceptance of these projections means that a great many nuclear plants must come into operation soon—the equivalent of more than a hundred of the giant 1-million-kwe size in the 1970s alone.

The fission process that runs present nuclear power plants is based on uranium-235, an isotope making up only 1 part in 140 of naturally occurring uranium.* Uranium-235 is unique among the several hundred naturally occurring isotopes in its property of *fissioning* (splitting) spontaneously into fragments if it "captures" a slowly moving free neutron. The splitting is accompanied by the conversion of about a tenth of a percent of the original mass of the uranium nucleus into energy, with the conversion factor being given by Einstein's famous formula, $E = mc^2$. The energy of fission appears as energy of motion of the reaction products. This fission process would be only a laboratory curiosity were it not for the fact that among the reaction products are additional neutrons—an average of 2.5 per reaction. These can lead to the fissioning of more uranium-235, the production of still more neutrons, and so on—the chain reaction that makes fission bombs and reactors work, yielding from a pound of uranium-235 the energy equivalent to burning three million pounds of coal.

In addition to naturally occurring but relatively scarce uranium-235, two man-made isotopes are also capable of sustaining fission chain reactions. These isotopes are uranium-233 and plutonium-239. They can be produced in quantity by bombarding the "fertile" isotopes, thorium-232 and uranium-238, with neutrons. Since uranium-238 and thorium-232 are hundreds of times as abundant in nature as uranium-235, they offer vast potential as a source of fission energy—provided only that the neutrons needed to convert them to "fissile" isotopes can be cheaply and safely supplied. The most prolific source of neutrons available is the fission reaction itself. A considerable amount of plutonium is produced routinely by the interactions of neutrons and uranium-238 in conventional fission reactors. Historically,

---

*An *element* is characterized by its atomic number, which is the number of protons in the nucleus. Most elements have several *isotopes;* these have the same atomic number, but different numbers of neutrons in the nucleus and hence different atomic weights. In the term uranium-235, "uranium" identifies the element and "235" specifies the isotope, being the total number of protons and neutrons in the nucleus.

most of this plutonium has been stockpiled in nuclear explosives.

It is possible to build a reactor that converts fertile ura-
nium-238 or thorium-232 into fissile fuels faster than it
consumes fuel for itself. This is the goal of the *breeder
reactor* program. A reactor in which significant conversion
of fertile into fissile material occurs is called a *converter*
if it does not meet the self-refueling criterion of the breeder.
It is called a *burner* if the conversion rate is very low. Today's power reactors are almost all burners, managing to
use only 1 to 2 percent of the energy available if the uranium
could be bred and consumed completely.

Adequacy of Fuel Supply

Great urgency has been ascribed to the breeder reactor
program on the grounds that the supply of uranium-235 for
use in conventional burner reactors is sorely limited. Actually, as we have already seen in the case of fossil fuels, the
question of supply in the short term hinges on technology
and economics more than on how much material actually
exists.

Uranium occurs naturally as uranium oxide (U_3O_8), which
sells today for about $6 per lb. Known and probable U.S.
reserves of U_3O_8 available at $5-10 per lb., if used in burner
reactors like today's, could supply *all* U.S. electricity for 35
years if consumption were stabilized at the 1970 level. (Consumption will not be stabilized there, of course, but neither
will nuclear fission be providing all U.S. electricity in the
foreseeable future. The figures given are simply intended to
convey a feeling for the size of the resources.) Known and
probable U.S. reserves available at $10-30 per lb. would add
only 55 more years under the same assumptions, but those
in the $30-500 range would add an impressive 10,000 years.
Moreover, there is good reason to believe that vigorous exploration will lead to a substantial increase in reserves,
especially in the $10-$30 price range.

Most experts will argue that the very large amounts of

uranium estimated in the $30-$500 price range cannot be taken too seriously because $500 per pound is roughly 100 times the price now being paid for uranium oxide for reactor fuel. Indeed, some people have claimed that $8 per pound is as much as reactor operators can afford to pay and still compete with fossil fuels. This narrow view fails to take into account the rising costs of fossil fuels and the cost of pollution control that in the future will be required on fossil fuel plants. It is simply impossible to predict in 1971 acceptable fuel costs for nuclear plants in 1985 or 1995, but the figure could easily be $50 per pound of uranium oxide.* In fact, the cost of the raw uranium oxide is such a tiny fraction of the cost of nuclear-generated electricity that the seemingly astronomical $500 per pound figure would barely double the ultimate delivered cost of power. Evidently, the "uranium shortage" is very much a matter of one's economic assumptions.

It is also a matter of technological assumptions. The breeder reactor being touted as the only solution to extending uranium reserves would utilize 40 to 50 percent of the energy content of uranium, instead of the 1.5 percent assumed for conventional burners. Such a big step, however, is not necessary. If, for one reason or another, the advent of a safe and reasonably economical breeder reactor were delayed, it seems reasonable to expect that a generation of advanced converter reactors would fill the gap. If such converters could utilize just 5 percent of the energy content of uranium, the reserve figures given above would effectively triple.

All of this should not be taken as a defense of the present, inefficient burner reactors, nor as an attack on the breeder,

---

*At a 1.5 percent fuel utilization factor and 33 percent plant efficiency, U_3O_8 at $8 per pound contributes only 2/100's of a cent to the cost of a kwhe. Nuclear fuel costs 10/100's to 15/100's of a cent per kwhe, mainly because of the cost of enrichment and fabrication into fuel elements. These parts of the fuel cost are independent of the cost of the raw material. Thus an increase in the price of uranium oxide to $50 per pound would add just 1/10 of a cent per kwhe to the cost of electricity at the plant, or 7 percent to the present delivered cost of power.

e discussed later. We are simply arguing that
he breeder cannot be made on the grounds of an
ortage of uranium. Even more than is so with
the fossil fuels, absolute supply is simply not the immediate
issue in nuclear energy.

Radiation and Public Health

Radioactivity and Radiation. Most of the hazards associated with energy production from nuclear fuels involve radiation, so it is helpful to acquire some background on this
subject before considering the details of fission technology.
Radioactive substances are those whose atoms undergo spon-
taneous changes in nuclear structure—nuclear disintegration
—emitting energetic particles and/or penetrating electromagnetic waves in the process.* For reasons that need not concern us here, the particles and the waves are all considered
to be *ionizing radiation.* It is enough to know that the hazard
to organisms of ionizing radiation depends mainly on the
amount of energy deposited in tissue and the place it is deposited.

Amounts of radioactivity are customarily measured in
curies. A curie is the number of disintegrations occurring per
second in one gram of radium. Doses of radiation are measured in *rads* or *rem.* We will stick with the rad, which measures the amount of energy deposited per unit of weight of
the absorber. For most purposes the rad and the rem are
equivalent, and are used interchangeably. Because small
amounts of radioactivity and low doses of radiation are of
biological importance, the *microcurie* (one millionth of a
curie) and the *millirad* (one thousandth of a rad) are used
in many discussions.

An important property of any radioactive isotope is its
half-life, which is the time after which half of an initial num-

---

*The principal particles emitted are neutrons, helium nuclei (two protons
plus two neutrons) and electrons. In the context of radioactivity, the
helium nuclei and electrons are called alpha and beta particles, respectively. The electromagnetic waves, called *gamma rays,* are identical to
x-rays of equal energy in every respect except origin.

ber of atoms will have undergone radioactive disintegration. This means that three-fourths of the initial material has disintegrated after two half-lives, seven-eighths after three half-lives, and so on. It take twenty half-lives for an initial quantity of radioactive atoms to be diminished one million-fold, and one must plan on waiting at least this long before the quantities of many isotopes produced in a nuclear reactor can be considered innocuous. Some isotopes have half-lives measured in seconds or less, so they disappear quickly. Others, like cesium-137 and strontium-90, have half-lives of about 30 years, so that twenty half-lives amount to 600 years. And some must be considered dangerous essentially forever: plutonium-239 has a half-life of 24,400 years.

Effects on Health. Man lives—and has always lived—in a "sea" of ionizing radiation from which he cannot escape. Known as the *natural background,* this radiation comes from cosmic rays, from radioactive materials in the earth's crust, and from certain natural isotopes, such as potassium-40, that circulate in the biosphere. The natural background amounts to an average of .08 to .15 rad (80 to 150 millirads) per person per year. Because man has evolved with this inescapable background does not mean that it is safe, however, and it would be foolish to shrug off man-induced radiation exposures that happen to be smaller than the background or comparable to it. Indeed, there is no reason to doubt that a burden of genetic defects and cancers has always been associated with the natural background, and that additional radiation exposure that man brings upon himself will increase this burden.

Naturally, the effect of radiation on humans is most obvious where the dose is large. Acute radiation sickness results from doses of 100 rads or more, delivered to the whole body over short periods. Such doses are associated with the use of nuclear weapons or serious accidents in the handling of reactors and radioactive isotopes. A dose of 500 rads would result in the death within thirty days of 50 percent of the people receiving it. Large doses are known to be less devastating if spread over a long time, for the body has some capability to repair the damage.

The long-term effects of radiation exposure, even in small doses, are of three kinds: general life-shortening, production of cancer, and genetic damage (or mutations). The first two effects may not appear for decades; genetic damage appears only in subsequent generations. Science has not unraveled the exact mechanisms by which cancer is caused, or which lead to an average shortening of life (unattributable to specific causes of death) in laboratory animals exposed to radiation. It is clear that the incidence of these effects increases with the size of the dose, but there is not enough evidence to prove whether there is direct proportionality or some more complicated dependence on dose at the lowest levels.

Mutations are random changes in the complex DNA molecules that contain the genetic code—the instructions for the development and functioning of human beings. Most mutations are harmful, as are random changes in any other complex apparatus such as a computer or a TV set. If the mutation occurs in a cell that will produce sperm or eggs, the mutation may be passed on to future generations. Repair of genetic material by certain enzymes has been shown to occur, but the fact that many mutations *are* passed on shows that such repair processes are imperfect. Although the details are not understood, it is clear that repair processes do not solve the genetic aspect of radiation exposure.

Standards. Most standards for "permissible" radiation exposure originate with the International Commission on Radiation Protection (ICRP). As the name suggests, the ICRP is an international body of recognized experts on various aspects of radiation. Its recommendations are not binding, but the main ones are generally followed by the regulatory agencies in the various countries. (In the United States, the Atomic Energy Commission still is in charge of enforcing most radiation standards, although the power to set standards was recently transferred to the Environmental Protection Agency.)

The principal recommendations of maximum permissible

doses resulting from the peaceful uses of atomic energy are: 5 rads per year for workers in nuclear technology, ten times less (0.5 rads or 500 millirads per year) for any individual in the general population, and thirty times less (0.17 rads per year) as an average individual dose for large segments of the general population. These standards refer to radiation *in addition to* the natural background, and they do not include medical radiation. They do recognize that radiation doses must be assumed to be cumulative, so that the 0.17 rad figure, for example, reflects the intention to limit genetic exposure for large populations to 5 rads in the first thirty years of life.

These dosage figures are used as a basis for calculating a much wider variety of standards for the *maximum permissible concentration* (MPC) of the various radioactive isotopes in air and water, and for the permissible rates of discharge of such isotopes from nuclear power plants and related activities. Such calculations must account for the behavior of the different isotopes in the human body, for the manner in which some of them are concentrated in biological food chains, and for the effects of multiple sources of exposure.

The Present Controversy. The adequacy of radiation standards has been the subject of debate inside and outside the scientific community for many years, but the discussion was given a new intensity beginning in late 1969 by nuclear chemist John Gofman and biophysicist Arthur Tamplin of the AEC-supported Lawrence Radiation Laboratory in Livermore. Many issues have been raised in the ensuing controversy, some to be touched upon in our discussion of fission technology, but the main points raised by Gofman and Tamplin concerning standards were these:

1) The AEC, in its public relations activities promoting nuclear energy, has regularly implied that the permissible dose of 170 millirads per person for large groups of people represents a safe level of exposure. This implies that there is a threshold dose of radiation below which no damage is done—an assumption contrary to the position of the ICRP

and one for which no conclusive experimental evidence is available.

2) If the harmful effects of radiation do exist in direct proportion to the dose down to the lowest levels, as Gofman and Tamplin claim mounting evidence indicates, the scientists conclude that exposing everyone in the United States to the permissible dose would lead to at least 32,000 additional cancer deaths annually, to say nothing of genetic and other effects. Gofman and Tamplin have suggested lowering the permissible levels at least ten-fold.

Many other respected scientists have voiced warnings concerning low-dose radiation. Dr. Karl Z. Morgan, first U.S. member of the ICRP, argues that medical uses of radiation should be included in the 0.17 rad standard. Because the therapeutic and diagnostic uses of radiation in medicine now average 0.06 rads per person per year in this country (more than 90 percent of all man-made radiation exposure), this would reduce the allotment for nonmedical uses to 0.11 rads per year. Geneticist Joshua Lederberg of Stanford University has estimated that the ultimate health cost of radiation exposure, considering only genetic effects, is between $100 and $1,000 per rad per year. Using the intermediate figure of $500 per rad led the Nobel prize-winning geneticist to estimate that exposing 200 million Americans to 0.10 rads per year each would lead to an eventual cost, over a period of generations, of about $10 billion per year.

The response of the AEC and its supporters has been varied and sometimes inconsistent. Some spokesmen have continued to insist that there *is* a threshold, which seems an irresponsible gamble in the absence of proof and in the face of some evidence that there is not. (For both sides of this controversy, see *Environmental Effects of Producing Electric Power* and *Poisoned Power*.) The AEC has also argued that 5 rads delivered over thirty years is not as dangerous as 5 rads delivered all at once—an assumption that is plausible only for damage that the body can repair. We do not even know what the specific nature of some of the damage is, so the AEC's argument here seems to be another dangerous gamble. To the AEC's claim that the health costs of radiation exposure are outweighed by the benefits of the uses of nuclear energy, Gofman and Tamplin and many others reply that this decision should be made by the public, not by the promoters of nuclear technology.

Finally, the AEC has pointed out that the public is not receiving today more than a small fraction of the permissible dose of nuclear energy, and that the AEC does not intend to expose large segments of the population to 0.17 rads per year in the future. For the first situation we can be thankful. As to the future, why should the AEC be so reluctant to give its good intentions the force of law by lowering the official standards? As this is written, the AEC has finally announced that it will reduce its standards for emissions from certain kinds of nuclear reactors one hundred-fold. Although this is a gratifying step in the interests of public health, it it important to note that the overall standards for human exposure will remain unchanged. As we shall see in the next section, the technology of fission power involves potential releases of radioactivity at many stages other than at the reactor itself.

Technology and Its Impact

Exploration, Extraction, and Processing. The impact of exploration for uranium deposits is relatively minor, involving only drilling for core samples and perhaps some invasion of wilderness areas by men and equipment. The mining and processing of uranium ore, on the other hand, are much less innocuous. Where it occurs near the surface, uranium is mined by open pit methods; otherwise conventional underground mining techniques are employed. Open pit mining, like strip mining for coal, scars the landscape and creates a disposal problem of removed surface materials. Miners in underground uranium operations must brave most of the same poor working conditions and safety hazards as coal miners do, and they are exposed to dangerous levels of radioactivity as well.

The principal source of mine radiation exposure is radioactive radon gas (resulting from the radioactive decay of actinium, one of the decay products of uranium-235) which tends to remain in the mines because it is much heavier than air. Radon is thus breathed directly by the miners, and the solid decay products of radon (called *radon daughters,* and also radioactive) are not only breathed but also tend to remain in the lungs. The result has been a significantly higher death rate from lung cancer among uranium miners than that of the general population or among other miners. The government study, *The Economy, Energy, and the Environment,* reports, "There is some disagreement whether it is possible or economically feasible to reduce radon exposure to the levels set by the Department of Labor." If, indeed, it proves technically impossible to reduce radon exposure to the point where incidence of lung cancer among uranium miners is the same as in the rest of the population, one might ask whether underground uranium mining is *morally* feasible. If achieving the needed reductions is simply a matter of having to pay more for uranium, then this is just one more economic cost that reasonable men must weigh when comparing alternative energy sources.

One point essential to such a comparison between coal and uranium is that considerably less material is involved per kwhe in the case of uranium. Nevertheless, the difference is not as large as the energy contents of these fuels would indicate, because only 0.2 percent of the uranium ore being mined today is recoverable U_3O_8, only 85 percent of the U_3O_8 is uranium, and only 1 to 2 percent of the uranium is actually fissioned in present reactors. All things considered, it takes fifty to one hundred times less uranium ore than coal to yield 1 kwhe under today's conditions.

Two-tenths of 1 percent U_3O_8 in the ore means four pounds of U_3O_8 per ton. The process of extracting those four pounds at a uranium mill results in 865 gallons of liquid wastes, which are both chemically toxic and radioactive. The solid wastes from the processing at the mills resemble sand and are called *tailings.* The handling of both the liquid and solid wastes from uranium mills has been and is a travesty. For years, liquid wastes were simply dumped into the streams of the Colorado River Basin where most U.S. uranium is mined and processed. In the late 1950s it was discovered that residents of several cities downstream were receiving from 1.5 to 3 times the ICRP's maximum permissible intake of radium—one of the most dangerous of all radioactive isotopes—because of these irresponsible procedures *(The Careless Atom; The Economy, Energy, and the Environment)*. Even today, exposures are one-third of the "permissible" levels.

Solid tailings have usually been piled near the mills, where they are exposed to erosion by wind and rain. Some 30 million tons of tailings have now accumulated. Those at abandoned mills alone contain enough radium to exceed considerably the maximum permissible body content of this substance for every man, woman and child on the planet. Some of the piles are situated adjacent to population centers; most are beside rivers and streams. Worse yet, the smallest tailings particles, which are the most susceptible to being washed or blown away, contain the highest concentration of radium.

Perhaps the most incredible debacle of the uranium mining and processing situation was revealed in 1970: some 3,000 homes in Grand Junction, Colorado, have been built on land fill consisting of uranium mill tailings. We are assured that the matter is "under study"; in the meantime, 3,000 families are breathing air contaminated with a still undisclosed amount of radioactive radon gas which emanates from the radium underlying their yards and porous concrete foundations. The half-life of radium is 1,620 years.

From Uranium Mill to Reactor. The volume of raw uranium leaving the mills in the form of U_3O_8 is not large because it is only about 1/500 of the weight of the original ore, and because the ore, in turn, is only 1/70 of the weight of its energy equivalent in coal.

Although the uranium oxide is radioactive, it is much less so than the fission products that must be transported later. Also, unlike the tailings, the economic value of the U_3O_8 is high, so it is handled carefully. Thus the losses in transportation are small, and its hazards are fewer than those at the other stages of producing energy from fission. The U_3O_8 does not go directly to the nuclear reactors, but rather to enrichment plants operated by the AEC. There the concentration of the fissionable isotope, uranium-235, is increased several-fold over its 0.7 percent occurrence in natural uranium. The residue of this process is depleted uranium containing about 0.2 percent uranium-235. The enriched uranium is shipped elsewhere, again at relatively low risk of environmental harm or damage to health, to be fabricated into fuel elements for reactors.

Reactors are not supplied with fuel day-by-day as are fossil fuel power plants; a 1-million-kwe reactor begins operation with an initial charge of some hundred tons of enriched fuel, which is replaced at an average rate of about thirty tons per year during the life of the plant. Transportation of new fuel thus becomes a rather sporadic matter consisting of only a few shipments per year. This is a considerable advantage over coal plants: a large one typically requires two large, noisy trainloads of coal per day to stay in operation, and pays a high economic price for this fuel transportation. On the other hand, the transportation of spent fuel elements away from nuclear reactors poses difficulties and hazards that compensate for the ease with which the fuel arrived.

The Reactor Itself. The basic scheme by which electricity is generated in a nuclear power plant is identical in most respects to that of a fossil fuel plant. The main difference is that the heat source for turning water to steam is a nuclear reactor rather than a furnace fueled by coal, gas or oil. Heat is generated in the reactor by the fission reactions themselves, and by the subsequent radioactive decay of some of the reaction products. Once this heat energy has been used to make steam, the steam spins a turbine that drives a generator, just as in a fossil fuel plant.

The main components of the reactor itself are the fuel,

the moderator, the control rods and the coolant. The fuel, the moderator and the control rods constitute the *reactor core,* which is contained in a steel reactor vessel. This arrangement is shown schematically in Figure 4. The function of the moderator is to slow down the energetic neutrons produced by fission so that they will be captured by uranium-235 to sustain the chain reaction. (Recall from the discussion of fission physics above that only slow neutrons cause uranium-235 to fission.) Without a moderator, a reactor fueled wtih uranium enriched to only 2 or 3 percent uranium-235 would not function because so many of the fast neutrons would escape from the reactor or be captured by uranium-238 without causing fissions. Ordinary water and graphite are two good moderators.

The control rods must be made of a material, such as cadmium or boron, that absorbs (catches and holds) neuttrons very readily. To make the fission chain reaction run faster, the control rods are partly withdrawn from the reactor core so that fewer neutrons are absorbed and more are available to cause fissions of uranium-235. To slow down the reaction, the control rods are moved deeper into the core, making fewer neutrons available to cause fissions. In this way the reactor can be made to produce power at any given level up to its design capacity. In the event of a malfunction, or a maintenance shut down, the control rods are pushed all the way into the core so that the chain reaction is quenched by neutron starvation.

The function of the coolant is to carry the heat of fission and radioactive decay away from the core. Without the coolant, the core would get hotter and hotter until the fuel and supporting structure melted. In most present power reactors, ordinary water serves as both coolant and moderator. These are called *light-water reactors* to distinguish them from those in which heavy water* is used as moderator and/or coolant. Light-water power reactors are futher divided into *boiling-*

---

*Heavy water is D_2O, where D stands for deuterium, a nonradioactive isotope of hydrogen having a proton and a neutron in the nucleus instead of only a proton.

water reactors (BWRs) and *pressurized-water reactors*
(PWRs). In a BWR, the water serving as a coolant is turned
to steam in the reactor. In a PWR, the cooling water is maintained under such great pressure that, no matter how hot it
becomes, it cannot turn to steam. The heated pressurized
water leaving the reactor core is passed through a heat ex-
changer, where its heat is used to make steam from water
circulating in a separate closed cycle. The BWR and PWR
cycles are shown schematically in Figure 5. Of the fifty-eight
commercial power reactors in operation or under construction in early 1970, twenty-one were BWRs and thirty-four
were PWRs. Two were gas-cooled, graphite-moderated reactors, in which a gas turbine rather than a steam turbine is
used to drive the generator; one was a fast breeder.

Nuclear reactors have the great environmental asset of
producing no air pollution of the usual kind—no oxides of
sulfur and nitrogen, no ash, not even any carbon dioxide.
They also require less land than a coal-fired plant of the
same capacity, since no coal storage yard or ash disposal
area is needed. But they have several liabilities that must
be weighed against these assets: the procurement of their
fuel involves special problems already discussed; they generate more on-site thermal pollution than modern fossil
plants of the same electrical capacity; they routinely release small amounts of radioactivity to the air and water;
a possible major accident could release much larger quantities of radiation to the environment; and they produce concentrated radioactive wastes that must be isolated from the
biosphere for centuries.

That reactor power plants generate more waste heat per
unit of electrical output is precisely the definition of lower
thermal efficiency. The reason reactors are thermally less
efficient is that they do not produce steam at as high a temperature as a fossil fuel plant does, and efficiency is crucially
dependent on the maximum temperature in the steam cycle.
The maximum temperature in any plant is determined by the
point at which metals and other materials making up the
equipment start to lose their strength. The materials in a

nuclear reactor must contend with damaging bombardment by radiation as well as with high temperature, so they weaken at a lower temperature than they would if temperature were the only factor. This aspect of the problem can and probably will be remedied by technical innovation, so that advanced nuclear plants of the future will have thermal efficiencies comparable to fossil fuel plants. Neither this nor any other technical remedy will solve the thermal pollution problem completely, however, as discussed in Chapter 5. The environmental effects of thermal pollution and the means of lessening them are covered there.

When an atom of uranium-235 splits, the possible products include a wide variety of fission fragments, in addition to the inevitable neutrons. Many of these fission products are highly radioactive; other fission products and structural materials that are not radioactive to begin with become so when bombarded by the fission neutrons. Fortunately, most of the fission products remain bound up in the fuel elements, which are clad in alloys resistant to heat and radiation, along with the uranium-238 and unfissioned uranium-235. Nevertheless some escape to the cooling water which is flowing between the elements, and others reach the air inside the reactor vessel. Additionally, impurities in the cooling water may become radioactive from bombardment by neutrons. A certain amount of radioactive gas from the reactor building is routinely released to the atmosphere, usually from a tall stack, and water from which some but not all of the radioactive contaminants have been removed is mixed with cooling water from the condenser and discharged to the environment. (Note that the water that passes through the condenser and carries off the waste heat from the steam cycle is not the same water that cools the reactor—see Figure 5.)

In principle, the most serious problems in routine reactor operations are the radioactive gases, krypton-85 and tritium (the customary name for the isotope, hydrogen-3). Krypton is an inert gas and so cannot be removed chemically. Tritium is difficult to handle because it diffuses readily through metal and because it tends to replace the hydrogen atoms in water.

Other more dangerous isotopes—for example iodine-131, cesium-137, and strontium-90—reach the reactor's cooling water if the metal cladding on a fuel element breaks. Such fuel element failures, resulting from the combined effects of heat and intense radiation, are so common that it is reasonable to call a certain number inevitable at the present "state-of-the-art." Under pressure from concerned scientists and other citizens, reactor manufacturers are hastening to develop what they call "zero-release" systems to capture and hold all radioactive isotopes inside the reactor building. In practice, of course, there is no such thing as zero release of anything, but the attempt to approach this ideal is admirable.

The basis on which the AEC regulates the routine emissions from nuclear power plants is that an individual breathing the air on the plant boundary twenty-four hours a day would not exceed the allowable radiation dose of 0.5 rad per year, nor would an individual taking all his drinking water from the reactor's effluent exceed this dose. This method is said to be conservative because no member of the public is actually expected to do either thing. It is not obvious, however, that the concentration in food chains of some of the isotopes has always been correctly considered—for example, the concentration of cesium-137 in fish may be several thousand times that in the surrounding water. Another potential difficulty is multiple sources of exposure, such as several reactors located in a single river basin, for a given population. In principle, biological concentration and multiple sources must be considered when setting standards, but the complexity of such calculations may encourage laxity and errors.

In practice, most reactors today release far less radioactivity than the regulations allow—the latest plants are designed to release 100-fold less under fairly adverse conditions (1 percent of the fuel elements damaged). Many have achieved release rates considerably lower than this. Conceding that such performance is obviously technically feasible, the AEC has finally agreed to assure that it is delivered by lowering the official guidelines for emissions from light-water reactors 100-fold.* Two plants that have been releasing some isotopes at 20 to 50 percent of the old guidelines will be given several years to comply. Both offenders are BWRs, which, in general, have substantially higher emissions than PWRs. A major reason is that the primary coolant, which becomes radioactive, has access to much of the rest of the plant by virtue of being the same water that circulates in the steam cycle (see Figure 5).

As if to compensate for its emission characteristics in routine circumstances, the BWR is inherently safer than the PWR from accidents that could release far larger amounts of radioactivity. There are two reasons for this. First, the pressure throughout the primary coolant system—hence inside the reactor—is higher in a PWR than in a BWR. Second, the boiling water in the core of the BWR is an inherent safety factor because any tendency of the chain reaction to "run away" makes the water boil faster; the extra bubbles reduce the effectiveness of the water as a moderator and the reaction slows down.

In both kinds of reactors there are many other devices designed to prevent or contain a major accident. These include automatic shutdown devices, provision for emergency cooling if the primary coolant should be lost, auxiliary electric power systems to keep pumps and safety devices running in the event that other available power is shut off, and, if all else should fail, a containment vessel constructed to withstand the largest explosion the designers regard as possible. An explosion like that of a nuclear bomb is *not* possible because the "bomb-grade" uranium-235 is so highly diluted with uranium-238. Nevertheless, any accident that led to a large-scale melting of fuel could result in a large steam or chemical explosion. It is against such a possibility that the containment vessel is designed.

In the judgment of the AEC and reactor manufacturers, these precautions make a major reactor accident—one in which large amounts of radioactivity are released to the

---

*This would correspond to .005 rad per year at the plant boundary.

environment—extremely improbable. Unfortunately, the consequences of this improbable accident could be enormous. Thus we are confronted with what Dr. Edward Teller (not known as an opponent of nuclear power!) has called "the zero-infinity dilemma": the probability is near zero, but the consequences are nearly infinite. For example, a single 1-million-kwe power reactor contains, after a year of operation, 1,000 times as much radioactivity as was released in the atomic bomb dropped on Hiroshima. The release of all or any significant part of this radioactivity to the environment as the result of an accident that breached the containment vessel would be an unprecedented disaster. A widely quoted 1957 AEC study ("Theoretical Possibilities and Consequences of Major Accidents in Large Nuclear Power Plants") calculated that such a major accident, for a considerably smaller reactor than those being built today, could (in the worst case they postulated) kill 3,400 people, injure 45,000 and do $7 billion in property damage. This study has caused the AEC so much grief that they have declined to update it to correspond to new knowledge and larger reactors placed closer to cities. However, a study at the University of Michigan, relating to the Fermi fast breeder reactor thirty miles from Detroit, concluded in 1957 that the worst possible accident there could kill 133,000 people outright.

Numbers such as these call for rather careful reflection on just how improbable such an accident really is. Unfortunately, no one can say for sure. It is argued that some 650 reactor-years of commercial experience have been accumulated in the world without a major accident. However, this shows only that the probability of a large accident is unlikely to be as high as one accident per 100 reactor years. One major accident per 1,000 reactor years as an average probability cannot yet be ruled out on the basis of actual experience, and it is also unclear how much of this experience is really relevant to the much larger reactors now coming into operation. The AEC projections for the production of nuclear power would require about 1,000 reactors in operation in

1990—which means that if the accident probability were one per 1,000 reactor years, we could then expect one accident somewhere in the United States *every year.*

Again, no one knows what the chance of a major accident actually is, and reassurances that cite very tiny probabilities must be taken with a grain of salt. Highly improbable events have a way of happening anyway in complicated technological systems, as the 1965 Northeast power blackout, the sinking of the "unsinkable" Titanic, and the failure of other "fail-safe" and "fool-proof" systems have demonstrated. A number of distressing accidents in experimental nuclear reactors have actually occurred *(The Careless Atom),* fortunately with little consequence to the public. Moreover, inspections and tests of safety systems for commercial power reactors have periodically revealed worrisome flaws—for example, hairline cracks in concrete containment vessels, and most recently, evidence that the emergency cooling systems on many U.S. reactors might not work at all *(Science,* May 28, 1971).

Convincing answers to certain other questions of safety do not seem to be available. Even if a containment vessel could withstand the force of a large steam explosion, could it withstand the armor-piercing effect of the large, sharp fragments of piping and structure that such an explosion might hurl at it? How vulnerable are nuclear plants to sabotage? Can engineers who are unable to guarantee a freeway overpass against failure in a moderate earthquake guarantee a reactor building against failure in a large one?

One can argue, of course, that the complexities of reactor safety make this a difficult area for judgments by laymen or scientists trained in other fields. But it is revealing that the western hemisphere's largest insurance companies (which can presumably afford competent advice) have refused, even as a coalition, to underwrite more than about 1 percent of the potential liability for the "maximum hypothetical accident" described in the AEC's 1957 report. Because no utility would operate a nuclear reactor without adequate insurance, the AEC and the Joint Committee on Atomic Energy of the U.S. Congress arranged an unprecedented maneuver: they persuaded Congress to pass in 1957, and to renew in 1967, legislation making the U.S. government liable for damages up to $478 million in a nuclear power plant accident. If such an accident occurred, a coalition of insurance companies would pay the first $82 million, the taxpayers would pay the next $478 million, and the victims would be uncompensated for any damages in excess of that. Recall that the AEC's own maximum damage estimate for a moderate-sized reactor was $7,000 million! This legislation, known as the Price-Anderson Act, thus deprives the public of its traditional last line of defense against industrial irresponsibility: in the past, when an activity was too risky to insure, it simply did not take place.

The solution to this problem is not giving up on nuclear power. It is reducing the price of the worst possible accident to the point where plants can be insured completely and without an act of Congress. Possibly the only way to do this is to place the plants deep underground, as many people have suggested. This would increase the price of nuclear power by a still uncertain amount. But as Professor David R. Inglis, a distinguished nuclear physicist, has so aptly put it: "We should ultimately have nuclear power when it is so much needed that we will be ready to pay for caution."

The Spent Fuel. Two of the most hazardous aspects of power from nuclear fission occur after the electricity has been generated: the reprocessing of the spent fuel, and the handling of the radioactive wastes from the reprocessing operation. After the fuel elements have been in the reactor for a year or two, they become so poisoned by the accumulated fission products that they must be replaced. *Poisoning* refers to the fact that the fission products absorb neutrons, which are then unavailable to keep the chain reaction going. When the fuel elements are removed, they still contain an appreciable amount of unfissioned uranium-235, as well as some fissionable plutonium-239. Fuel reprocessing consists of extracting these valuable materials from the array of incredibly radioactive fission products that accompany them.

This process takes place in a separate fuel reprocessing plant. The only such plant in commercial operation is located in upstate New York, although three plants are operated elsewhere under contract with the AEC. The first problem is transporting the spent fuel elements from the reactor to the reprocessing plant. This is done by rail or truck, in shipping casks weighing from 20 to 100 tons and holding between one and ten fuel elements each. The fuel elements are hot thermally as well as radioactively—the heat released by continuing radioactive decay of the fission products could easily cause the elements to melt—so the casks must be supplied with a self-contained cooling system. The casks are designed to withstand severe impacts, fire and immersion in water. Again, the chief question centers around the probability of a shipping accident severe enough to rupture such a cask. (The chance would seem to be low if the casks are as good as claimed.) We will have plenty of opportunities to learn the answer because even the largest cask must make about seventeen trips per year to service a 1-million-kwe reactor.

Once at the reprocessing plant, the fuel elements are chopped into pieces and the contents dissolved in acid for chemical separation. At this point the barriers between the concentrated radioactive material and the environment are at their lowest, for now the protection afforded by the metal and ceramic cladding of the individual, solid fuel elements is gone. Virtually all of the operations at the reprocessing plant must be conducted by remote control because of the intense radiation emanating from the wastes. Many of the gaseous and liquid effluents are controlled using scaled-up versions of the systems used at reactors. Thus, most of the krypton-85 and some iodine-131 goes up the stack, while essentially all of the tritium comes out in the waste water. Reports filed by the operators of the New York plant say that it has been operating at 10 to 30 percent of the officially permissible discharge rates for most substances, but in some instances has exceeded the permissible levels for short time periods. Independent investigators from the University of

Rochester claim that the concentration of radioactive isotopes in the creek that drains the vicinity of the plant has considerably exceeded permissible levels. The AEC's new agreement to lower emission standards specifically excludes reprocessing plants.

The residue remaining after reprocessing is a concentrated witch's brew of radioactive wastes which boils continuously because of the heat generated by its own radioactive decay. Present processes produce 100 gallons of this high-level liquid waste per ton of spent fuel processed. These wastes contain about 50,000 curies of fission products per gallon, 1,000 curies of which is strontium-90. The maximum permissible concentration of strontium-90 in a public water supply is less than a billionth of a curie per gallon.

At the present time, these liquid wastes are stored in underground steel tanks, each with its own cooling system, at the same location as the reprocessing plants themselves. No high-level liquid waste is shipped. The great proportion of tanks now in existence are situated at weapons-related facilities in Hanford, Washington; Idaho Falls, Idaho; and Savannah River, South Carolina. (Most reactors in operation prior to 1960 were used mainly to produce plutonium for the manufacture of nuclear bombs.) The AEC and everyone else knows that the underground tanks are only a temporary expedient for waste storage because corrosion will eat the tanks away far sooner than the six to ten centuries minimum that the wastes must be interred. Indeed, 10 of the 149 tanks at Hanford have already developed leaks: more than 200,000 of the 74 million gallons stored there have seeped into the ground.

The AEC has proposed, as a long-term solution, that the high-level wastes be solidified into a glass-like material, and that this be buried deep in natural salt deposits—the idea being that salt deposits are free of ground water that might dissolve the wastes and permit them to reenter the biosphere. Additionally, salt is a good conductor of heat, which is essential if the waste is not to melt its way straight down and away from its intended place of confinement. The AEC has acquired an abandoned salt mine in Lyons, Kansas, as its first such burial ground. However, scientists at the Kansas Geological Survey and many other Kansans are not convinced that the AEC has shown its plan to be safe. They are concerned about the possibility that wastes will migrate out of the salt deposit, that earthquakes will let water in, and that there may be accidents in transporting and handling the wastes. Whether the salt mines are the final answer to the very difficult problem of high-level wastes remains to be seen.

Less concentrated but still dangerous radioactive materials are also created at many stages of nuclear power production, and these, too, constitute a waste disposal problem. As discussed above, some of the less concentrated gaseous and liquid wastes are discharged to the environment. Contaminated solid materials are usually merely buried in trenches ten to fifteen feet deep and covered with soil. Such practices have presumably been adopted because they are cheap, not because more responsible alternatives do not exist. A study of radioactive waste disposal practices made by the National Academy of Sciences concluded (as summarized in *Resources and Man*): "In fact, for primarily economic reasons, practices are still prevalent at most Atomic Energy Commission installations with respect to these [low-level] categories of wastes that on the present scale of operations are barely tolerable, but which would become intolerable with much increase in the use of nuclear power."

A final waste problem is the question of what to do with the reactor itself after its useful life of twenty or thirty years has ended. At the present time, it is said to be uneconomical to dismantle the intensely radioactive reactor completely, and the method of disposal is entombment in concrete on the site. As nuclear physicist George Weil has put it: "Thus a decision today to build a nuclear power plant is a decision to dedicate the reactor site as a permanent monument—a legacy to future generations to maintain hazard-free."

Economics and Subsidies

The term *economies of scale* refers to the fact that cost per kwhe decreases for both fossil fuel and nuclear power plants as plant size increases. The comparative economies of scale of coal and fission plants are such that fission becomes really competitive (in parts of the country where coal is not too expensive) only in very large plants—say, of 400,000-kwe capacity or more. For this reason, a whole generation of very large nuclear plants is being built without the large backlog of experience in operating smaller plants that was accumulated in the more gradual development of the fossil fuel industry. This in itself could lead to problems of reliability in the large nuclear plants, which would make their power more expensive than is now being claimed. A nuclear plant must operate reliably and at high load factor for twenty years if the cost per kwhe is to be as advertised. In 1969 only three nuclear plants of more than 400,000-kwe capacity were in operation (the oldest having gone into service in 1967). Yet forty-four plants of more than 400,000 kwe—a dozen of which are to be larger than 1 million kwe—were then under construction.

Construction costs quoted for nuclear plants have risen dramatically from the neighborhood of $135 per kwe of capacity in 1960 to $210 in the late 1960s, to $310 for plants scheduled to go into service in the years 1976-77. Part of this increase has been created by inflation, but construction costs for fossil fuel plants have not risen as fast. A rough estimate is that construction costs per kwe for plants on which work is now beginning are 20 to 40 percent higher for nuclear than for fossil plants. Nuclear plants are said to compensate for this difference with their lower fuel costs. The costs of electrical transmission and distribution are the same for either kind of plant, assuming that both are permitted to operate at the same distance from the places electricity is consumed. Thus, the total cost of electricity under current assumptions about pollution control is the same—about 1.5 cents per kwhe.

Nuclear energy has enjoyed several hidden subsidies, the importance of which is difficult to evaluate in numerical terms. One is the matter of accident insurance discussed above. Utilities must pay for their $82 million worth of coverage from the insurance industry but not for the $478 million worth from the taxpayers. If they did have to pay for all of it, and the premium were the same, only 3/100's of a cent per kwhe would be added to the operating costs. However, because the potential damage is not $560 million but more than $7,000 million, the *effective* subsidy is much larger than this. It is the amount the utilities would have to pay in improved reactor design or siting to make themselves legitimately insurable, and nobody knows how much that is.

Another subsidy is the considerable amount of research and development money the AEC has applied to the present generation of power reactors. Prior to 1971, all commercial power reactors in the United States were licensed and built as experimental devices, thus permitting the use of AEC research funds. After years of steadfast refusal, the AEC has finally agreed to declare reactors of commercial value, a belated and reluctant concession to the obvious fact that they are being sold and operated as profit-making items for the manufacturers and the utilities.

The AEC's policy of buying back the unfissioned plutonium-239 produced in today's reactors and recovered in reprocessing the fuel has also been regarded by some as a subsidy. The market price of plutonium is fixed by the government—some think unreasonably. The rebate to the reactor operators is about 10 to 15 percent of their fuel costs, or 1 percent of the delivered cost of power.

Regulation and Conflict of Interest

Many disturbing questions surround the proliferation of fission power plants, and new ones arise with the proposed widespread introduction of breeder reactors into the power grid (Chapter 6). If these questions are to be resolved in the public's interest and to the public's satisfaction, it will re-

quire conservative standards, uncompromisingly enforced, by
a body whose only interest in nuclear power is protection of
the public. The Atomic Energy Commission is not and cannot be such a body because it is entrusted with two incom-
patible roles: the promotion of the peaceful uses of nuclear
technology, and the regulation of this technology. Regardless
of the good intentions of the men involved, it is asking too
much of anyone to be promoter and regulator at the same
time. And it is asking too much of the public to accept such
a conflict when the risks are so high.

The dual role of the AEC was an operating necessity in
the years immediately following 1946 when the commission
was established. At that time, the only individuals possessing
the knowledge to be regulators were the scientists and admin-
istrators working on the cutting edge of nuclear energy programs. Today the necessary knowledge is much more widely
disseminated, and the dual role has outlived its usefulness.
That the philosophy of the role of the commission has not
changed with the times is most evident in the backgrounds of
the five commissioners themselves: an economist, a nuclear
engineer, a biochemist, and two attorneys.* Where are the
ecologist, the medical doctor, the specialist in public health?
They are on the advisory committees, but their absence at
the highest level says a great deal about the relative importance of promotion and regulation in this body.

The supposed watchdog over the AEC is the Joint Committee on Atomic Energy (JCAE) of the U.S. Congress. The
hearings of this committee over the years are a valuable
source of information on many aspects of nuclear energy,
but for checks and balances the public will have to look
elsewhere. The joint committee and the commission have
evolved a cozy, cooperative relationship over the years, with
the promotion of nuclear technology as their common goal.
Anyone who doubts this need only refer to the JCAE's

---

*In July, 1971, President Nixon named an economist and an attorney to
replace retiring Chairman Glenn Seaborg, a nuclear chemist, and the late
Theos Thompson, a nuclear engineer.

hearings on *Environmental Effects of Producing Electric Power* of late 1969 and early 1970. In these 2,700 pages, the reader will find JCAE Chairman Chet Holifield (multi-term congressman from southern California) and his colleagues consistently badgering and belittling witnesses critical of the AEC and its standards, while coddling the commissioners themselves and praising with fatherly approval the testimony of witnesses supporting the status quo.

If the AEC and the JCAE wish to be as successful in the future as they have been in the past in promoting electric power from fission, they would do well to surrender their standard-setting *and* enforcement functions to a regulatory agency independent of either body. An informed and responsive public would be foolish to settle for less.

5. Energy Use, Thermal Pollution and Climate

Localized effects on aquatic life;
large-scale effects; altering climate.

Until recently, heat was rarely considered a pollutant. Engineers worried about ways to improve the efficiency of electric power plants because they wanted to get more electricity out of a pound of fuel, not because of the environmental effects of energy wasted as heat. This casual attitude about thermal effects was prevalent for two reasons. First, the amount of energy that man introduced into his environment in any one place was rarely large enough to cause any important biological disturbance. Second, the total amount of energy manipulated by man was small compared to the large-scale natural energy flows that govern climate. The first situation has changed because of economies of scale—in order to generate electricity cheaply, we have made generating plants larger and larger, finally reaching the point where the waste heat discharged from a single one may be a significant perturbation in the local environment. This local problem is the one most people think of when they hear the words "thermal pollution."

The second situation also is changing, and the result also deserves to be called thermal pollution. The combined effects of population growth, increase in per capita consumption of energy, and urbanization have led to a situation in which man's manipulation of energy is becoming comparable to some of the energy flows affecting climate. Today this is true only in cities, but, if present trends continue, it will be so over much larger regions by the turn of the century. The problem is that all energy consumption—from metabolism to driving an automobile—results in the production of heat. In the case of a power plant, the heat delivered to the environment includes not just the waste heat at the site but virtually all of the useful output as well: the electricity itself is transformed into heat in wires, light bulb filaments, the bearings of electric motors, and so forth. The fact that all the energy we use is eventually degraded to heat is another consequence of the second law of thermodynamics.* Neither technological gimmicks nor scientific breakthroughs can be expected to change this fact. Ultimately, the wholesale thermal pollution associated with energy consumption will reach the point where it must be stopped by stabilizing both population and per capita consumption. Of course, other problems may have this effect before thermal pollution does.

Man also has the potential to influence climate on a large scale through the release of large quantities of carbon dioxide and particulate matter, of which major sources are the generation of electricity and other forms of energy consumption. Here, man affects climate by changing the balance among natural energy flows, rather than simply by adding heat energy to the system. These are large-scale effects, so they will be treated along with large-scale thermal pollution in what follows.

Local Thermal Pollution and Aquatic Life

Power plants that operate with steam cycles, whether the basic energy source is coal, gas, oil or fission, give up waste

---

*Most of man's energy use, probably more than 95 percent, is converted to heat immediately, as in the friction of automobile tires against pavement or the hot exhaust from an air conditioner. A small fraction is stored, as when energy is used to remove the oxygen from iron ore (Fe_2O_3). In this example, the energy would ultimately be released as heat when the iron rusted back to Fe_2O_3.

heat when steam is changed to water in the condenser. The waste heat is transferred to the condenser coolant, for which the most economical and practical choice is water. By far the cheapest approach to disposing of this waste heat is called *once-through cooling:* taking the cooling water from a river, lake or body of salt water, passing it once through the condenser, and discharging it to the original source some ten to twenty degrees Fahrenheit warmer than it began. A fossil fuel plant operating at a power level of 1 million kwe and an overall efficiency of 40 percent will warm about 30 million gallons of water per hour by fifteen degrees Fahrenheit. A nuclear plant delivering the same amount of electricity and operating at 32 percent efficiency causes the same temperature rise in about 50 million gallons of water per hour. This corresponds to the entire flow of a moderate-sized stream. The thermal discharge to water from the nuclear plant is higher not only because the efficiency is lower, but also because the fossil plant disposes of some of its waste heat directly to the atmosphere via the stack.

The seriousness of the environmental effects of thermal pollution has been the subject of considerable controversy, and some people have suggested that the term be changed to "thermal effect" or even "thermal enrichment." On balance, however, the bad effects considerably outweigh the good. Temperature is the most important governing factor in aquatic biological processes. As water temperature increases, the metabolic rate of aquatic animals goes up and they require more oxygen. Unfortunately, the ability of water to hold dissolved oxygen decreases as temperature increases; thus, while the animals need more oxygen, there is less available. Up to a point, as long as there is sufficient oxygen, increasing water temperature raises the rate of growth of aquatic life. This may be desirable in the case of some food species, but many have been shown to reach greater size, although at a slower rate, in colder water. Because different species of plants and animals have different optimum temperatures, a change in the average temperature of a body of water usually leads to a change in the species that predominate. More often than not, less desirable species are favored by warm water—carp replace bass and trout, and algae and aquatic weeds thrive. Warm water also apparently increases the incidence of disease among fishes. Some migratory fishes seem to use water temperature as an indicator of when to move upstream to spawn; they may be deceived by thermal pollution and come to grief when conditions upstream are not those needed.

Many of these problems are compounded because the power plants are not discharging a constant amount of waste heat. The water temperature will fluctuate with the plant's load factor. Thus shutting down the plant completely for maintenance purposes (or, in the case of a reactor, refueling) will cause a sudden temperature drop perhaps even more damaging than the previous rise.

Man suffers directly from aquatic thermal pollution when important food and sport fishes are decimated, when algae and weeds make recreational uses of the water less appealing, and when the high algae content of drinking water makes supplies difficult to purify. The diminished oxygen content of the warmed water causes it to assimilate less of the other waste products of man and his industries, so odors, scum, and further fish die-offs occur at rates of waste input that could otherwise be tolerated. Increasing the temperature of water also increases the rate of evaporation, with two effects: less water is available for use downstream, and minerals already present in the water tend to become concentrated. These problems may become appreciable if water from a single river flows successively through several power plants on its way downstream. In a few instances, of course, thermal discharges may help keep a navigable river ice-free in winter, or make swimming possible in a body of water that would otherwise be too cold. But these seem rather small benefits to be weighed against the adverse consequences that are likely to follow in the majority of cases.

The waste heat discharged into a river, lake or ocean is eventually transferred in the natural course of events to the atmosphere. (As a body of water gets warmer, the rate at which it transfers energy to its surroundings increases). All the methods for alleviating the impact of aquatic thermal pollution consist of ways to get the heat into the atmosphere without warming a natural body of water in the process. One method being used by some utilities is the construction of artificial cooling ponds. These typically must cover 1,000 to 2,000 acres of land for a 1-million-kwe plant, which compounds the difficulty of finding a suitable site. Also, depending on the location, there may be more desirable uses for the land. A regular supply of water must also be available to make up for losses by evaporation.

An approach already widespread in Europe and gaining favor in this country is cooling towers, of which there are several varieties. In a wet cooling tower, the heated water from the power-plant condenser falls through an upward-moving stream of air and is cooled mainly by evaporation. The air may be forced through the tower by fans (mechanical-draft tower) or by forces arising from the shape of the tower and the humidity inside (natural-draft tower). The discharge of water vapor to the atmosphere by evaporation in a wet tower typically amounts to several million gallons per day. This may be enough to cause ground fogs and frosts, and the consumptive use of water is a drawback. Air currents carry off droplets of water in addition to water vapor. These droplets may contain chemicals previously added to the water to prevent plant growth in the cooling system, chemicals resulting from corrosion, and minerals that have been concentrated within the system. A dry cooling tower avoids these shortcomings by circulating the water through an elaborate array of closed passages so that no water is lost; the heat is transferred to air flowing over and around the passages much as in the radiator of an automobile. Dry cooling towers are by far the most expensive means of transferring waste heat to the atmosphere; most of those in operation are outside the United States and all are on relatively small power plants. All cooling towers, and particularly the natural draft variety, share the esthetic drawback of great size. A natural draft wet tower may be as large as 600 feet in diameter at the base and 500 feet high. Such a structure dominates the landscape for many miles.

Estimates of the costs of building and operating cooling towers and cooling ponds vary considerably. The construction costs seem high—$10 to $20 per kwe for cooling ponds or wet towers, perhaps $30 to $60 per kwe for dry towers. Nevertheless, even when the extra operating costs are accounted for, the total increase in the delivered price of electricity is not large. It ranges from 0.5 percent for cooling ponds to possibly 10 percent for dry towers (*Scientific American,* May 1971; *The Economy, Energy, and the Environment*).

In principle, a more logical approach to the problem of waste heat from power plants is to put it to good use. In some cities in northern Europe, the warm effluent is used to heat apartments and office buildings. This option is practical and economical only if the power plant is located in the heart of a large concentration of population. There are obvious drawbacks, however, to siting fossil fuel and fission power plants in the midst of cities—pollution, safety and land prices. Again, putting nuclear plants underground might offer a solution. Research has indicated that some kinds of crops grow better when irrigated with warm water, which may offer an alternative for power plants adjacent to farmland. In the case of condenser effluent from nuclear plants, this use, and the related one of accelerating the growth of shellfish, might call for even tighter restrictions than at present on the concentration of radioactive isotopes in the water. It is also possible to use some of the waste heat from seaside power plants for desalting sea water. Large dual-purpose plants providing both electricity and fresh water have been proposed but none has been constructed. The outlook for using warm condenser effluent in other industrial processes is not bright because the concentration of the heat energy— its temperature—is so low. Near urban areas, the waste heat eventually may be used to speed up bacterial decomposition of sewage.

In all the alternatives just described, the end result is the dissipation of energy to the atmosphere. Putting the heat to practical use on its way to the atmosphere has the advantage (at least in the cases of space heating and desalting) of conserving other energy resources that would otherwise be applied to these tasks.

Large-Scale Effects

Waste heat reaching the atmosphere by one or the other of the routes just described is simply one component of a man-made thermal burden that eventually includes all useful energy consumption as well. To understand the effects of this heat, one must look first at the natural energy flows that cause the phenomena we perceive as climate. The temperature at the earth's surface is determined by the balance of energy that comes in and energy that goes out. Of the solar energy hitting the top of the atmosphere, some is reflected off clouds and dust and returns directly to space, some warms the atmosphere, and some reaches the surface of the earth. Of the amount reaching the surface, some is reflected and some is absorbed—mainly by warming the surface and by evaporating water. Energy that takes the second pathway is later released to the atmosphere when the water condenses and falls as rain.

The balance between energy striking and leaving the earth's surface is maintained by a simple physical principle: as a material body gets warmer it gives off heat energy to its surroundings at a faster rate. (Recall that the rate of energy flow is *power*.) Therefore, any increase in the input of power to the earth's surface causes the surface to warm up until the additional rate of heat outflow balances the additional input. Any decrease in the input causes the surface to cool until the power in and power out are again in balance. Such up and down temperature fluctuations occur in any given place from day to night and from summer to winter. Local climates also depend strongly on the differences in solar input with latitude, on the winds and ocean currents that result from these differences, and on the way the winds and ocean currents are affected by geographical features and by the rotation of the earth. On a yearly average over the whole globe, however, almost exactly as much energy as enters the earth-atmosphere system is returned to space, either as direct reflection of solar energy or as heat.

An average power balance for the entire earth is shown in Figure 6. Dotted lines denote flows that would not occur in man's absence. Notice that the power that man taps from the fossil fuels and from nuclear sources is a net addition to the global balance, rather than a mere diversion of an existing energy flow. (For example, the half-life of uranium-235 is so long—713 million years—that for practical purposes no energy at all comes from it unless man splits it in his reactors.) Hydroelectric power and harnessed solar power, by contrast, are not thermal polluters in the global sense because this energy would have been converted to heat at the same rate even if man had not tapped it.

Man's energy consumption can affect these large-scale processes on several levels. The climate of large cities, where most of the energy consumption takes place, differs appreciably from that of the surrounding countryside. Cities are warmer (by an average of about a degree), wetter (5 to 10 percent) and foggier (30 to 100 percent). Many factors are involved, some not directly related to energy consumption, but the release of heat from human activities and the haze of pollutants from burning fossil fuels are certainly important ones. Over the 740 square miles of the Los Angeles Basin, the thermal power from man's activities is equal to more than 5 percent of the solar power reaching the surface.* In the near future, such situations will become regional rather than local, and the results may be much more harmful. Projections using current growth rates show that, by the year 2000, man's power input over 11,000 square miles of the Boston-Washington megalopolis will be equal to 50 percent of the solar power reaching the surface in

---

*Data courtesy of Professor Lester Lees of the California Institute of Technology.

winter, and 15 percent in the summer. Man's knowledge of
the complexities of the meteorological system is too small
to predict what the result will be, but very substantial and
serious changes are possible. We seem intent on finding out
by experiment.

Some people have made the reassuring claim that we will
not be in serious climatological difficulty until man's power
consumption is at least 1 percent of the solar power reaching the entire surface of the globe. It would be foolish to
bet on this: the meteorological processes that govern climate
should probably be regarded as a finely tuned engine, in
which east-west, north-south, and up-down energy flows
which are much smaller than the total solar input play criti-
cally important roles. Man's power input will continue to be
unevenly distributed, and could easily swamp some of the
critical natural processes over large regions well before the
1 percent of solar level is reached globally. As a reference
point, though, it is sobering to discover how quickly even
the 1 percent level (200 times today's consumption) could
be reached: if the current growth rate in world energy consumption of 5 percent per year continues, we will be there
in about 100 years.

Carbon dioxide and water vapor, seemingly the most innocuous combustion products from fossil fuels, may also
have serious effects on climate. Both substances have the
property of being essentially transparent to incoming solar
energy, but partly opaque to outgoing heat energy. They
intercept some of the outbound heat flow that would otherwise escape to space and redirect it back to the surface. This
constitutes an increase in power input to the surface, which
must therefore warm up to restore the balance. We should
be grateful for this property of naturally occurring carbon
dioxide and water vapor (called the *greenhouse effect* because glass has similar properties) because without it the
average temperature on the surface of the earth would be
about ten degrees below zero, Fahrenheit.

The concentration of water vapor in the atmosphere as a
whole does not seem to have been much affected by man.

The water vapor produced in burning fossil fuels stays relatively close to the surface of the earth, and, while it may have local effects, is on the whole a small factor compared to water vapor moving through the natural hydrological cycle. Carbon dioxide, by contrast, mixes throughout the atmosphere—measurements show that its concentration globally increased by about 10 percent between 1890 and 1970. Much of this increase apparently came from the combustion of fossil fuels, although some may have come from newly cleared farmland and from natural sources. Elaborate calculations indicate that continuing present trends in fossil fuel consumption could lead to an increase of 1.4 degrees Fahrenheit in the average surface temperature of the globe by the year 2000 *(Man's Impact on the Global Environment)*. These calculations have not taken into account the effects of such an average increase on the atmospheric circulation patterns that really govern regional and continental climates. It is important to understand that these effects could be much more dramatic than a mere 1.4-degree temperature change would seem to imply.

Dust, smoke, and other forms of particulate matter in the atmosphere can also affect climate. The most obvious effect is reflection of incident sunlight away from the earth's surface, causing cooling which might counter-balance the effect of the carbon dioxide increase just described. There is some evidence of a slight global warming trend between 1900 and 1940 and a cooling trend since; some people ascribe the combination to the greenhouse effect in the first period, with cooling due to atmospheric dirtiness becoming dominant after 1940. However, it is now known that particles in the atmosphere can cause cooling *or* warming at the surface, depending on their type, size and altitude. Moreover, particles can come from agricultural burning and other farming activities, forest fires, and volcanoes, as well as from burning fossil fuels. It is believed that volcanoes are the most important source at the present time, but man's contribution is rising steadily. Obviously, no definitive prediction about the effects of particulate pollution on climate is possible at the present time. These are matters we should know more about before permitting many additional doublings of energy consumption.

It might be asked why we should worry about man-made changes in climate at all, since climate has been changing naturally for millennia. The difference is that we are now obliged to worry about the welfare of the world's very considerable human population. A drop of only a few degrees could bring on a new ice age that might cover much of the world's most productive cropland with glaciers; a rise of a few degrees could melt the icecaps and raise sea level by 150 feet, flooding coastal plains and their cities. Any rapid change in climate will disrupt agriculture, which depends on plants that are highly adapted to specific growing conditions. Such prospects sound remote, and they are—compared to the oil spills, poisoned urban air, threats from nuclear accidents and waste, and the rest of the legacy of energy consumption *today*. These more immediate problems, and others associated with providing a rising standard of living for an endlessly growing population, seem likely to force a halt before we succeed in disrupting climate on a large scale. Nevertheless, those who concede no limits at all to man's ability to manipulate nature should look into meteorology and climate more closely. For if nothing else stops us, these problems will—although no one can yet say exactly when. We could be most unpleasantly surprised if atmospheric circulations prove susceptible to a cascading, growing domino effect of some sort (known in the trade as an *instability*), in which an unwitting contribution by man at some leverage point in the system leads to a disproportionate and catastrophic result.

6. Energy Supply Tomorrow

Fission breeder reactors; fusion; solar energy; geothermal, tidal and wind energy; burning garbage; advanced conversion.

Today's sources of energy leave much to be desired. While some of their drawbacks can be remedied without drastic changes, the solution of man's energy problems in the longer term must rest with sources different from any discussed so far. In the near future, as well, it is possible that new sources —or old ones that were previously of minor importance— will rise to prominence as technical, economic, and environmental factors change.

What are the characteristics of a better energy source? If it is to be of much importance, such a source must be able to sustain a high rate of use for a long period of time. (A few sources, such as hydroelectric and tidal energy, meet the second part of this criterion but not the first; they are virtually inexhaustible, but the rate of use, or total power output, is limited by the number of exploitable sites and rate of energy flow in the hydroelectric and tidal systems.) A better energy source would minimize disruption of the environment and of human health in extracting and transporting the fuel, and would be clean and safe in use. If a source could be used to produce electricity more efficiently than today's methods do, in the sense that less energy were wasted at the site of generation, this would also be desirable. Low cost in an energy source would make it particularly attractive to underdeveloped countries. In industrial nations, on the other hand, cheapness of energy as a goal in itself has been overemphasized; in fact, many environmental problems have been caused or aggravated by energy already being too cheap.

The principal contenders to bear the brunt of man's energy consumption in the long haul seem to be only three: the fission breeder reactor, the fusion reactor and solar energy. Sources which may be important in some locations, in descending order of probable contribution to the energy budget, are geothermal, tidal and wind energy. Finally, the efficiency of electrical generation may be improved within the framework of present *or* future energy sources by advanced techniques for conversion: at present, magnetohydrodynamics (MHD) and fuel cells are the most promising.

FISSION BREEDER REACTORS

A breeder reactor produces fissionable fuel from nonfissionable raw material in sufficient quantity not only to refuel itself but also to fuel other reactors as well. This does not mean that a breeder reactor gives us something for nothing, or that it is a perpetual motion machine of sorts. It must be continuously supplied with the specific nonfissionable raw material that is transformed to fuel inside the reactor. The two raw materials capable of being transformed in this way are uranium-238, which constitutes 99.3 percent of natural uranium, and thorium-232, which constitutes essentially all of natural thorium. Both these substances are found in scattered deposits of high-grade ore and in common rocks such as granite and shale. Although these rocks may contain only 50 parts per million by weight of uranium or thorium, this is enough to make a pound of rock equivalent, in theory, to 150 pounds of coal.*

---

*Because today's reactors utilize so little of the energy content of natural uranium, we are getting only the equivalent of 70 pounds of coal per pound of the high grade uranium ore now being mined.

Assuming that a practical and safe breeder reactor is developed, it is likely to be some time before mankind will be reduced to using common rock for his energy source. The point, say the breeder people, is that the rock will be there when man needs it, and there is enough in the first thousand feet or so of the earth's crust to satisfy an energy demand much larger than today's for thousands of centuries. The difficulties of crushing the rock and extracting the uranium and thorium should not be underestimated, and the chemical and mineral residue—if this were the dominant source of energy for the world—would be staggering. Nor is the prospect of grinding up New Hampshire's Conway granites and California's Sierra Nevada for fuel a pleasing one. Nevertheless, if civilization should last so long and if no better energy source were available, it would be done.

How They Work

Breeder reactors are made possible because the splitting of fissile substances (uranium-235, plutonium-239, uranium-233) produces more neutrons than are needed to sustain the chain reaction. In an ordinary burner reactor, the excess neutrons are absorbed by the control rods, the fission products in the core, and the structural materials of the reactor. In a breeder reactor, the idea is to use the excess neutrons to bombard the fertile materials, uranium-238 and thorium-232, and thereby transform these into fissile plutonium-239 and uranium-233. The time it takes a breeder reactor to double its initial inventory to fissile fuel by this means is called its *doubling time,* and is expected to range from seven to twenty years.

There are two basic kinds of breeder reactors being investigated in the United States today: the *liquid metal fast breeder reactor* (LMFBR), which operates on the uranium-238 to plutonium-239 transformation, and the *molten salt breeder reactor* (MSBR), which uses the thorium-232 to uranium-233 transformation. The main difference in physics between the two systems is that the LMFBR fuel cycle requires fast (high energy) neutrons to succeed, while the MSBR cycle proceeds with slow or thermal neutrons. This distinction means that the two kinds of reactors are technically very different, and it has important safety ramifications. The vast bulk of U.S. research on breeders has been concerned with the LMFBR so we will concentrate on it here.

The breeding ratio (fertile atoms converted divided by fissile atoms consumed) exceeds 1 in the LMFBR's uranium-plutonium fuel cycle only if most of the neutrons produced can initiate fissions or transformations before being slowed to low energies. The reactors designed to meet this requirement have a very compact core of highly enriched uranium-235 or plutonium, and they have no moderator. A fast breeder reactor actually contains more fissile material than a conventional (thermal) reactor producing the same power, and this material must be crammed in more concentrated form into a much smaller space. This makes the fast breeder reactor inherently more difficult to handle and potentially more dangerous than a conventional reactor.

Because the fission energy in a breeder is produced in a very compact volume, a very efficient coolant is required to carry this energy off. This and the additional requirement that the coolant be a poor moderator of neutrons leads to the choice of liquid sodium. This material has the advantage of carrying off great quantities of heat with no rise in pressure; it has the disadvantages of becoming intensely radioactive in the reactor core, and reacting violently with water so as to release hydrogen gas, which is itself explosive. Obviously, great care must be taken to keep the radioactive liquid sodium, which is circulating at temperatures between 750 and 1,000 degrees Fahrenheit, well shielded and away from water. Typically, three different closed fluid circuits are involved, as shown in Figure 7.

Several safety features inherent in present light-water reactors (BWRs and PWRs) are necessarily missing in the fast breeder. The high power density in the breeder core means that, in the event of a blockage or pump malfunction in the cooling system, the fuel melts much faster. Because the fuel is not nearly as dilute as in a conventional reactor, melting that does occur is far more likely to lead to the unanticipated assembly of a *critical mass*—the amount of fuel that can sustain a chain reaction on its own. In a light-water reactor, unwanted temperature increases in the core tend to be counterbalanced because the efficiency of the water moderator decreases as its temperature increases; in a fast breeder, there is no moderator to provide this insurance. Moreover, control of the fast breeder is made especially difficult by the short neutron lifetime—the neutrons do not have to bounce around and slow down before causing a chain-reaction-sustaining fission, as in a conventional reactor. Finally, for reasons we will omit in the interest of brevity, a reactor fueled with plutonium is slightly more difficult to control than one fueled with uranium-235. Although the first fast breeders will use uranium-235 as the initial fuel, the entire fast breeder energy economy will eventually be running on plutonium-239.

Not only do accidents seem more likely to occur in a fast breeder reactor, but also those that might occur seem more likely to breach the reactor vessel and containment structure. One reason is the extra chemical explosive energy represented by the liquid sodium. Another is the possibility of a "secondary" accident involving the fissionable material in the core, such as rapid fissioning of a critical mass of melted fuel sending shock waves surging through the rest of the core—just the right combination of intersecting shock waves might hold a critical mass together elsewhere long enough to give an explosion that could shatter any envisioned containment vessel. The likelihood of such an accident is the subject of dispute. The fact is that no one has been able to calculate what the absolute maximum explosion is, so no one can say whether it could be contained. Frank Farmer, head of the Reactor Safeguards Division at the United Kingdom Atomic Energy Agency's Health and Safety Division, recently wrote in the trade journal *Nuclear Safety:* "I believe that it will never be possible to prove that a fast reactor, or any other reactor, can be absolutely contained."

An accident that occurred at the first commercial LMFBR might have been expected to cause second thoughts among the promoters of the headlong rush toward fast breeder reactors. It apparently has not. This took place at the Enrico Fermi fast breeder reactor, built about thirty miles from Detroit as a "demonstration" project by the AEC and a coalition of utility and manufacturing interests. The maximum hypothetical accident at the Fermi reactor could kill 133,000 people outright, according to a 1957 study performed for the reactor's sponsors by the University of Michigan. The accident that did occur in October of 1966 killed no one, but it put the reactor out of commission for nearly four years. In partially melting two fuel subassemblies, it exceeded the "maximum credible accident" specified in the official AEC Hazards Summary for this reactor. The accident was stopped from proceeding even farther when radiation alarms in the reactor building convinced the operator to shut the reactor down by fully inserting the control rods. (It is interesting to note that the reactor was *not* shut down by automatic safety devices.) At the time, no one knew what had caused the accident, and one person present later reported the possibility of a secondary accident to have been "a terrifying thought." It took more than two years to complete the investigation which revealed what had happened: two pieces of sheet metal that had been added to the reactor system as an afterthought, and which did not even appear on the final blueprints, had been torn loose by surging liquid sodium, and blocked the flow of coolant to part of the core.

Fortunately, the Fermi accident did not lead to a secondary explosion, and little radiation escaped the reactor building itself. Under the circumstances, this outcome must be attributed partly to good luck. The entire matter is a commentary not only on the difficulty of ensuring safety in a fast breeder, but also on the responsibility of the promoter-regulators who permitted this highly experimental and very dangerous device to be built so near a major population center. The Fermi reactor resumed operation on July 18, 1970.

A problem that would be greatly aggravated by an energy economy relying heavily on breeder reactors is that plutonium-239 (like uranium-233 and -235) can be used to make bombs. In conventional reactors, the fuel is so diluted with uranium-238 that it could not be used to manufacture bombs without very sophisticated and expensive additional processing. It would not be as difficult to make a crude bomb from the plutonium-239 produced and used in fast breeder reactors, and there is great concern that a sufficient quantity could easily fall into the hands of criminal elements, revolutionaries, or unstable and unpredictable foreign governments. Even now the AEC seems unable to keep track of the plutonium it handles with an accuracy of better than about 1 percent (*Science* magazine, April 9, 1971). If 1 percent of the plutonium the AEC estimates will be circulating in the year 2000 went astray, it would be enough to manufacture more than 1,000 Nagasaki-size bombs.

Some of the problems enumerated here for the LMFBR are shared by the molten salt breeder; others are not. Molten salt is not as reactive as sodium, and the use of slow neutrons makes the reactor easier to control. On the other hand, the core is still relatively compact, and the uranium-233 on which the cycle runs could be diverted to make weapons. The main reason that the LMFBR has received more attention is that the molten salt reactor cannot double its fuel inventory as rapidly.

In other respects, all breeder reactors have liabilities similar to those of today's water-cooled reactors. They generate the same intensely radioactive wastes that must be processed and then interred for centuries. They require the same care to keep routine emissions of radioactivity to a minimum (and at the higher operating temperatures of breeder reactors, this may be more difficult to achieve); the amount of radioactivity released to the environment in a catastrophic accident would be equivalent to that from many fission bombs.

The advantages of breeders are that the fuel supply is nearly infinite if grinding up granite and shale can be managed, and that the power plant efficiency should be comparable to modern fossil fuel plants, thereby reducing local thermal pollution below levels typical of today's reactors. It has also been claimed that power from breeders will be relatively cheap, although this is not obvious. Fuel costs should be low, at least for some time to come, but construction costs are uncertain. The technology of breeders is elaborate and sophisticated; it has proved difficult enough to predict construction costs ten years in advance for the simpler water-cooled reactors. The breeder reactors that the AEC wants to put into operation in the mid-1980s will be fifteen times bigger than the Fermi plant (the largest with which we have any experience), but possible economies of scale are likely to be offset by needed safety measures such as building the plants underground.

The AEC and the present administration claim that we need large commercial breeders by 1985 lest inefficient water-cooled reactors use up all our uranium-235. But this prognosis is based on an unduly restrictive view of acceptable fuel costs. The public should not be rushed into a major commitment to breeders until it can be proved that they will be safer and cleaner than other options. Ultimately, they may be, so research money for the breeder reactor program is a wise investment. But undue haste in actually deploying this tricky technology is unnecessary and dangerous.

FUSION REACTORS

The sun, the stars, and the hydrogen bomb are powered by thermonuclear fusion. In this process, energy is released when the nuclei of light elements fuse together to form heavier ones, rather than by the splitting apart of heavy nuclei as in fission. The most suitable fusion fuels here on earth include the heavy isotopes of hydrogen (deuterium and tritium), the light isotope of helium (helium-3), and lithium. One of the main attractions of harnessing fusion power is the abundance of the fuel. The fusion reaction likely to be harnessed first would use deuterium and tritium.

Deuterium is easily extracted from sea water; tritium can be obtained from lithium, also present in sea water, by means of neutron bombardment in the fusion reactor itself.* Lithium is in shorter supply than deuterium, but there is enough in the seas for the deuterium-tritium reaction to supply all the world's energy for 120 million years at the 1968 level. If the fusion reaction that requires only deuterium could be harnessed, the sea could provide energy for the same number of years at almost forty times the 1968 level.

Fusion has important advantages in addition to its vast potential fuel supply: sea water from which the deuterium and lithium have been removed can be put back into the ocean with no ill effects; all fusion fuels and reaction products except tritium are nonradioactive; a fusion reactor would be inherently safe against nuclear runaway accidents; and it may be possible to convert the energy from fusion directly to electricity at very high efficiency (without a steam cycle), thereby greatly reducing thermal pollution at the power plant.

How They Work

Unfortunately, great technical difficulties stand in the way of harnessing fusion in ways other than thermonuclear explosions. Three conditions must be met. First, the fuel must be heated to a temperature of tens to hundreds of millions of degrees. Under such conditions, the fuel has reached the fourth state of matter (the first three being solid, liquid and gas), or plasma state: a gas in which all the particles are electrically charged, the electrons having been stripped off their atoms by the force of energetic collisions of one atom with another. Second, the heating to these extreme temperatures must be accomplished at a sufficient density of fuel particles so that collisions leading to fusion are frequent. Third, the hot plasma must be confined under these conditions for a time sufficient to obtain more energy from fusion than had to be contributed to heating and confining the

---

*The production of tritium in this way is somewhat analogous to the transformation of uranium-238 to plutonium in a fission breeder reactor.

plasma in the first place. Simultaneous achievement of these three conditions has eluded scientists throughout the world ever since serious work on the problem began about 1950. Nevertheless, steady progress has been made toward the goal, considerably aided by the unusual degree of international cooperation made possible by the multilateral lifting of all security restrictions on controlled fusion work in 1958.

Fusion is so much harder to achieve than fission because fission reactions are initiated by neutrons, which, being electrically neutral, easily penetrate the cloud of electrons surrounding the nucleus. Fusion reactions depend on bringing two nuclei into much closer proximity with each other than their associated electrons ordinarily permit, a process which requires stripping off the electrons and then bringing the nuclei together with enough force to overcome the repulsion of their like electrical charges—thus the requirement of high temperature.

In a hydrogen weapon, a fission bomb is used as a trigger to generate the needed temperature and density. Obviously, this won't do as a routine means of producing electric power. We must work with much lower densities, and, to compensate, hold the material together for a much longer time. In the sun and other stars, hot plasma is held together by the gravitational force of the star's great mass. This will not work on earth, either. Nor can we use a container in the usual sense of the word, because the hot plasma would be cooled immediately by contact with it. The most extensively explored route to harnessing fusion relies instead on the fact that electrically charged particles can be controlled and confined by magnetic fields. The object has been to devise "magnetic bottles"—complicated configurations of electromagnets —which can hold the plasma away from material surfaces and keep the plasma from escaping. So far, plasmas have shown a dismaying tendency to leak from the magnetic bottles faster than predicted; the enterprise has been aptly likened to trying to hold watery jello in a cage of rubber bands. Nevertheless, we are improving. An up-to-date description of research in this field, including promising efforts to dispense with the magnetic bottle by bringing pellets of fuel to fusion conditions instantaneously with a laser, is given in an article in the February 1971 issue of *Scientific American.*

The more optimistic fusion researchers believe that a demonstration of scientific feasibility (simultaneous achievement of the necessary temperature, density, and confinement time) will be achieved in the late 1970s or early 1980s if adequate federal research support is forthcoming. Once feasibility is demonstrated, a considerable amount of additional time presumably will be required to develop a practical fusion reactor for the power grid. The past history of such developments makes it unlikely that commercial fusion reactors will appear before 1990, or comprise an important fraction of total electric generating capacity before 2015. Of course, the speed with which fusion reactors are installed depends in part on their costs compared with alternative energy sources, and on how badly we want their environmental advantages. The end cost is uncertain; construction costs for a fusion reactor could be either higher or lower than, say, those of a breeder reactor. No one yet knows which controlled fusion route will succeed or what a fusion reactor will look like, let alone what one will cost.

Environmental Impact

Environmental and health hazards should be small compared to those of fission reactors but they will exist. The first generation of fusion reactors will almost certainly use the deuterium-tritium fuel cycle, in which the tritium is regenerated by the reaction of fusion neutrons with a lithium "blanket" surrounding the reactor. The inventory of radioactive tritium represents a biological risk, both from routine emissions and accidental release. The technology to control routine emissions of tritium, however, can certainly be developed. And if all the tritium were to escape, it would create a biological hazard about half a million times smaller than that of the iodine-131 in a fission reactor of equal

electricity demand projected for the future. They do argue, however, that it could provide electricity in many specific locations for a considerable length of time, with environmental advantages over many alternatives. Environmental problems with geothermal energy include the possibility of surface subsidence if the water is not pumped back underground, and noxious hydrogen sulfide gas that often accompanies the steam. Additionally, water from underground reservoirs is laden with mineral salts which could constitute a nuisance if not returned underground. The proposal has been advanced that, at seaside locations, waste heat from the generation process could be used to desalt ground water, with the residual brine (augmented by sea water) being pumped back into the ground to prevent subsidence. How all this would work out in practice remains to be seen. It is certainly worth pursuing.

Tidal and Wind Energy

The source of tidal energy is the gravitational force of the moon and the sun acting on the world's oceans. Like solar energy, this source will continue essentially forever. Exploiting the energy of the tides requires a partly enclosed coastal basin, the twice-daily filling and emptying of which can be harnessed by a dam containing two-way turbines. (Without a dam to create a difference in water level between ocean and basin, the force against the turbine would usually be inadequate.) The largest tidal power station now in operation is a 240,000-kwe installation in France. Unlike solar energy, tidal energy is wholly inadequate in magnitude to meet man's needs. All the exploitable tidal sites of the world together could provide an average total power of 13 million kwe, in the estimation of energy specialist M. King Hubbert *(Resources and Man)*. This amounts to less than 1 percent of the world's exploitable conventional hydroelectric power. Thus, while tidal energy may provide appreciable amounts of electricity with rather small environmental intrusion at specific locations, it will never contribute an important fraction of the energy consumption of this country or of the world.

Wind energy is even less promising, as there are few places in the world where the wind is strong enough and steady enough to make harnessing it for the large-scale production of power at all interesting. The ultimate source of the energy in the wind is the sun; the prospects for exploiting that directly seem much brighter.

Burning Garbage

Americans generate an average of five pounds of municipal solid wastes per person per day—not including industrial, mineral and agricultural solid wastes. The municipal wastes have a fuel value averaging 1.5 kwht per pound, or more than one-third that of high grade coal *(Environmental Cost of Electric Power)*. For many years the better part of the garbage from the city of Paris has been burned to produce steam for heating and for electric power plants. If all of America's municipal solid wastes had been used in this way in 1969 at 33 percent plant efficiency, they could have supplied about 12 percent of our energy consumption. A potential problem with this approach is the particularly noxious combustion products from the wide variety of plastics in municipal garbage.

Agricultural wastes are an even larger potential energy source. The amount of gas that could be extracted from the manure of farm animals in the United States each year would supply about 15 percent of this country's *total* energy consumption. The concentrated residue from this process would be a far more economical fertilizer than the original manure, and could partly replace inorganic fertilizers. Getting gas from manure, then, would help solve two problems at once.

ADVANCED CONVERSION

Most of today's electricity is produced by conversion from heat energy in a steam cycle, at an efficiency of 30 to 40 percent. This means that 1½ to 2 units of energy are wasted for every unit of electricity produced. Efficiencies of conventional steam plants may continue to increase slowly, but doing much better will require some basic changes of approach. The solid arrows in Figure 8 show the various energy transformations needed to make electricity in a standard plant, using a chemical fuel (not necessarily fossil) and a working fluid (not necessarily steam) that drives a turbine. Some of the total energy loss occurs at each such transformation; therefore a logical approach to increasing efficiency is to skip some steps. Some of the possibilities for doing so are indicated by the dotted arrows in Figure 8. A similar diagram could be made for production of electricity from nuclear energy; the only difference would be that the shortcut using the fuel cell is not possible when the source is nuclear.

Magnetohydrodynamics (MHD)

A conventional generator converts mechanical energy to electricity by forcing a copper conductor to move through a magnetic field. MHD generation bypasses the mechanical energy stage by making the working fluid itself a conductor of electricity and forcing *it* through the magnetic field. The usual method is to burn the fuel (*any* chemical fuel, including coal, gas or oil) at high temperature and to "seed" the combustion gases with a material, such as potassium or cesium, that is easily ionized (stripped of electrons) at these temperatures. The free electrons and positively charged ions make the combustion products a conductor of electricity. The hot, conducting gas is then expanded through a nozzle to high velocity, and passed through a channel to which a strong magnetic field has been applied. Direct current electricity is drawn off from electrodes lining the channel. Advantages of this system are simplicity, almost no moving parts, probably low construction costs, and (eventually) high efficiency.

Numerous experimental MHD generators have been built, and a vigorous research program—partly supported by utilities—is underway in this country to make them commercial. The first ones will supply peaking and emergency power. This means they will operate only during the several hundred or so hours per year when demand is exceptionally high, or in the event of breakdowns in the "base-load" equipment—conventional fossil fuel, nuclear and hydroelectric plants. Plants for peaking and emergency power need not be particularly efficient because they are not operating most of the time. On the other hand, such plants must be relatively cheap to build, be reliable and fast to start up. (It takes several hours to bring a fossil fuel or nuclear steam plant from a standstill to full capacity; an MHD peaking plant can do it in five seconds.) In the peaking role, MHD generators will compete with the gas turbine, which essentially is a jet engine driving a conventional generator. Gas turbine sales have increased dramatically since the 1965 northeastern power blackout demonstrated that emergency generating capacity in the United States is woefully inadequate. MHD generators and gas turbines share drawbacks of high production of nitrogen oxides, and high noise levels. Both discharge all of their waste heat into the atmosphere.

The first application of MHD to increase the *efficiency* of energy conversion will be in combination with conventional fossil fuel steam plants. In this application, called a *topping cycle,* the MHD generator exploits the fact that burning fossil fuel can produce higher temperatures than a steam or gas turbine can use. Such turbines have been limited because their blades must withstand both the high temperature of the input steam or gas and the enormous stresses of high speed spinning. But the hot gases in an MHD generator do not come in contact with moving parts, so much higher temperatures can be exploited. In a steam plant with MHD topping cycle, the exhaust gases from the MHD generator serve as the heat source that produces steam for the rest of the plant. Part of the electrical output comes from the MHD generator; part comes from the conventional generator in the steam plant. The overall plant efficiency of such a combination could be as high as 60 percent, thus reducing waste heat more than two-fold over today's most efficient plants.

MHD generators can also be used to "top" nuclear generating plants, but this is somewhat more difficult technically. In either case, substantial engineering problems remain to be resolved, so MHD topping seems unlikely to make a major contribution to raising plant efficiency before the 1990s. Ultimately, there may be very high-efficiency fossil fuel or nuclear power plants using purely MHD conversion, but this is much farther away.

Direct Conversion of Heat to Electricity

A number of physical phenomena are known in which heat energy is converted directly to electricity without even a working fluid as an intervening step (see Figure 8). One is thermionic emission, in which electrons can be made to boil off a suitable metal plate by heating it. In a device called a thermionic converter, this effect is exploited to produce an electric current. Another such phenomenon is thermoelectricity, in which a current is made to flow by heating the junction of two dissimilar metals or semiconductors. (This is how a thermocouple measures temperature.) Devices based on thermionic emission and the thermoelectric effect have been used to provide power in spacecraft, partly because they can be made quite simple and rugged. It is possible that similar devices will eventually be used for topping in combination with fossil fuel and nuclear power plants, but technical difficulties and high costs make such applications seem a long way off.

Fuel Cells

The fuel cell has the great attribute of converting stored chemical energy directly to electricity, skipping even the production of heat as an intermediate step. (*Waste* heat is produced because no such device can be completely efficient, but heat is not used in the direct sequence leading to the generation of electricity.) A fuel cell is identical in its principle of operation to an ordinary battery: a chemical reaction yielding electrons (oxidation) takes place at one electrode, and a chemical reaction consuming electrons (reduction) takes place at the other. The resulting deficiency of electrons at one electrode and excess at the other causes a voltage between them, and we have our source of electricity. The fuel cell differs from a battery only in that the reactants are continuously supplied from outside the fuel cell itself, and the reaction products are continuously removed.

Fuel cells can operate at higher efficiencies than conventional fossil fuel or nuclear power plants, they can be made to consume a wide variety of fuels, and they are not much more expensive per kwe in small sizes than in large ones. Fuel cells running on hydrogen and oxygen, and producing only water as the reaction product, have been extensively used to supply electric power on manned space flights. Other fuel cells run on natural gas, including gas produced from coal; a gas-powered model costing only $400 per kwe was recently demonstrated. At this price, individual home units to produce electricity efficiently, quietly and cleanly from gasified coal begin to be possible. As the price comes down —and researchers in this field unanimously agree it will— similar devices may become very attractive for powering automobiles. This is probably a decade or more away, and the remaining technical difficulties should not be underestimated. Nevertheless, the fuel cell is a very promising approach to more efficient and less disruptive use of our chemical fuels.

The fuel cell has the additional attribute of operating in reverse: by *supplying* electricity to the fuel cell, it can be made to convert reaction products back into reactants (for example, the electrolysis of water into hydrogen and oxygen). It happens that the hydrogen-oxygen combination is not very efficient in this respect, but others are. When the efficiency is high, the fuel cell becomes an attractive means of energy storage, to be used, for example, with solar energy as the primary source. Similarly, fuel cells can be employed to turn the output of massive fusion or fission reactors into a portable energy source.

7. Some Aspects of Demand

Population growth; energy and the economy;
demand versus need; implementing changes;
energy and the poor countries.

Knowing how energy is produced and what environmental costs accrue, we should try to determine why we are using so much energy, and whether the trends behind the forecasts described in Chapter 1 are really inevitable. Only by comparing the benefits of energy consumption with the environmental and human burdens can we begin to decide where such consumption ceases to be worth it.

Population Growth and Energy Consumption

What is the connection between population growth and energy use? Between 1880 and 1969, the population of the United States quadrupled while the total consumption of energy increased thirteen-fold. In the percentage terms often used in discussing these matters, the increase in population was 300 percent*; that of total energy consumption was 1200 percent. It is tempting to conclude from these numbers that population growth contributed only one-fourth of the increase

---

*A doubling is a 100 percent increase, a tripling 200 percent, and so on.

in consumption during this period, but this conclusion is not justified. Three hundred percent is simply the amount that energy consumption would have increased due to the observed increase in population, if *per capita consumption had remained at its 1880 value.* Per capita consumption did not remain there but, as some simple arithmetic shows, increased by 225 percent between 1880 and 1969. This 225 percent, then, is the amount that total consumption would have increased, due to the observed increase in per capita consumption, if population had remained at its 1880 level. Obviously, the individual percentage increases in population and per capita consumption do not add up to the total increase actually observed. Where did the rest of the increase —more than half of it—come from? It came from the multiplier effect of population growth and rising per capita consumption occurring simultaneously.

This argument is purely an arithmetical one, which does not account for the possibility that population growth and growth of per capita consumption of energy may affect each other. That is, depending on the circumstances, an increase in per capita availability of energy might actually *cause* either a rise or a fall in the rate of population growth. For example, energy-intensive medical services and sanitary engineering could lower the death rate and thus accelerate population growth, or improved education and availability of contraceptives could lower the birth rate and slow population growth.

Similarly, population growth itself can cause increases or decreases in per capita consumption of energy. For example, increases may arise because the complexity of such activities as transportation, communication and government expands disproportionately as population grows, and because of diminishing returns in providing the material ingredients of prosperity. Consider the problem of providing metals to a growing population. As the richest ores and those nearest centers of consumption are depleted, we are forced to use lower quality ores, dig deeper and extend our supply lines. In terms of mining, processing and transportation, this means more energy consumption per pound of metal (and thus, at a fixed level of affluence, more energy consumption per capita). Similarly, increasing food production on a fixed amount of land usually involves diminishing returns in fertilizer use: to raise yields by 50 percent may require tripling fertilizer input, and fertilizers consume energy in their production and distribution. As a final example, consider pollution control. If we find we must hold the total amount of some effluent constant as population doubles, then the per capita effectiveness of that particular kind of pollution control must double. Generally, this will mean twice as much investment of energy (or more) in pollution control, per capita.

Of course, improved technology and economies of scale postpone the onset of diminishing returns in some cases, particularly in manufacturing processes. Population growth may even diminish per capita consumption of energy in some activities if the larger population makes new and more energetically efficient processes feasible. Unfortunately, large industrial nations such as the United States seem to be well past the point where further population growth has such beneficial effects. Especially in the critical matter of supplying the raw materials of existence—food, water, metals, fibers—for a growing population, we have been using more energy per capita, not less.

Many individuals who have disparaged the importance of population growth in resource consumption and pollution seem unaware of the multiplier effect of population growth. They insist that population growth "caused" only one-fourth of the rise in energy consumption between 1880 and 1969, and leave it at that. The breakdown given above is more reasonable, although still not completely accurate because we do not understand all the ways in which population growth and per capita consumption of energy affect each other. Further work on this important relationship is badly needed. Nevertheless, even the simple arguments presented here are sufficient to show that population growth cannot be ignored as an important contributor to rising energy consumption. Clearly, whatever successes we have in stabilizing per capita consumption of energy, through more efficient technology and through more prudent energy use, will soon be canceled out by the sheer increase in the number of consumers if population size is not stabilized as well.

Energy and the Economy

Gross national product and energy consumption in the United States have increased at about the same rate for many years.* This fairly close parallel is not surprising because GNP automatically includes the complicated interactions of population growth, per capita consumption of goods and diminishing returns. There have been sufficient deviations in the ratio of energy to GNP, however, to show that the relationship is not ironclad, a view supported by examining the relationship in other prosperous countries. The four-fold variation in kwht per dollar shown in Figure 9 does not permit the pat conclusion that GNP is always proportional to energy consumption.

Energy promoters make a great deal of the fact that very low energy use is associated with very low GNPs in the poor countries of Asia, Africa and Latin America. For the purposes of deciding on an internal energy policy for this country, this observation is useless. After all, descending to the standard of living of India is not an option that the United States is considering. For us, the acid test of the assertion that prosperity is directly proportional to energy use is whether it holds in our "prosperity bracket." The answer is no.

Another way to evaluate the relationship between energy and the economy is to examine energy's contributions in dollars. The energy industries in this country generate about 4 percent of national income, the purchase of energy in the form of fuels and electricity accounts for about 7 percent of

---

*When consumption of fuel wood is included in the statistics, we find that energy consumption per unit of GNP increased slightly between 1880 and 1920, declined steadily but gradually between 1920 and 1945, and was nearly constant between 1945 and 1968. The net change in their ratio during the entire ninety-year period was remarkably small (*Energy in the United States*).

consumer expenditures, and the cost of energy represents less than 4 percent of the value added by manufacture in U.S. industry.* These percentages represent large amounts of money, but they do not indicate that an increase in the price of energy would cripple the economy, as some people have suggested.

If the link between energy consumption and prosperity is not as rigid as the energy promoters would have us believe, the link between electricity consumption and prosperity is even less so. As noted earlier, electricity must be produced from one of the more fundamental kinds of energy—solar, nuclear, fossil fuels, and so on. The rapid rise in electricity consumption is due in part to substituting electricity where fossil fuels once served directly (for example, in home heating and cooking). Such substitutions are not necessarily improvements in the standard of living. If they were, the electric industry would not have to advertise so vigorously to persuade people to switch.

For further evidence that there is no direct cause-effect relationship between electricity consumption and prosperity, we can look again to the international statistics of Figure 9. Norway has twice the per capita electricity consumption of the United States, and half the per capita GNP. Canada, too, has higher per capita consumption of electricity than this country and lower per capita GNP. The lack of an obvious relationship persists throughout the list.

Of course, GNP is a poor measure of true standard of living, both because of what it includes (for example, the cost of waging wars, the cost of crime) and because of what it does not (for example, the cost of the deterioration of our cities, now being paid not in dollars but in the inconvenience and misery of those who must live or work there). International comparisons are further hampered because official

---

*The term "value added by manufacture" refers to the difference between the value of the raw materials and that of the finished products. The contribution of energy is as high as 10 to 20 percent in a few key industries such as the processing of metals from ore.

currency exchange rates often do not reflect real purchasing power. These difficulties demonstrate that better indices of prosperity and quality of life are certainly needed. Nevertheless, it is likely that they would show the relationship between energy and prosperity to be even more tenuous than indicated in Figure 9, because the most deceptive per capita GNP shown is probably that of the United States (large military budget, high crime rate, unbalanced income distribution).

In the last analysis, one must ask whether further economic growth in a country such as ours is a desirable goal. If it is, ways could be found to permit such growth without energy consumption rising as fast as it is now. For example, the service sector of the economy produces more GNP per kwht than does the manufacturing sector. If economic growth itself is judged to entail more costs than benefits, as well it might *(Global Ecology)*, then any economic effects of stabilizing energy consumption would have to be considered an asset rather than a liability.

Demand Versus Need

The breakdown of U.S. energy and electricity consumption in 1969 is shown in Figure 10. To trace the flow of energy through society in much more detail than this is a complicated task and is not done routinely—perhaps the most definitive and reliable such analysis in recent years was done in 1963 in connection with the monumental study, *Resources in America's Future.* Part of the breakdown for 1960 is shown in Figure 11. Although these figures are now more than ten years old, the patterns of consumption change much more slowly than the magnitudes so the breakdown is probably still substantially accurate.

These are the sources of demand for energy, but a demand is not necessarily a need. One of Madison Avenue's main reasons for existence is to make us demand things we do not need. We have all seen these techniques applied to persuade us to use more energy. One reason such campaigns are successful is that energy is so cheap. Now we are discovering that all the costs are not being paid in dollars, but rather in human health, destruction of the landscape, and interference with the environmental systems that support life itself. It is therefore time to ask the hard questions: How much of our energy consumption is necessary? How much could energy consumption be reduced without seriously compromising real needs? A complete answer is impossible, but a detailed look at some of the major categories of consumption suggests that wasteful and frivolous energy use is rampant and that consumption per capita could easily be reduced.

Space Heating. Residential space heating accounted for 12 percent of total U.S. energy consumption in 1968. Experts declare that this amount could be reduced by one-third to one-half if homes were provided with proper floor, wall and ceiling insulation. Even the more expensive homes being built today are often deficient in insulation; less expensive homes almost invariably are. As a result, much of today's heating bill goes to heat the outside rather than the inside. If energy were more expensive, homeowners would be unlikely to let this wasteful situation persist.

Another aspect of this problem is the source of the heat. The trend, abundantly encouraged by advertising, is toward electricity; electric space heating of homes, stores and offices is a major component of projected increases in electricity use. Unfortunately, most of this is likely to be resistive heating, which means that the heat is produced by the electrical analog of friction opposing the flow of current through wires. The method is 100 percent efficient in converting electricity to heat, but very inefficient in terms of utilizing the energy of the original fuel. For every kwhe produced at a fossil fuel power plant, an average of 2 kwht is discharged to the plant's surroundings. By the time another 5 to 10 percent has been lost in transmission and distribution, the overall efficiency of resistive heating (defined as heat released in the house divided by the energy content of the fuel) is less than 30 percent. A typical home gas heater, by contrast, is 75 to 80 percent efficient, and quite clean. In terms of conserving energy, then, it is much wiser to heat with gas in the home than to burn more than twice as much fuel at the power plant in order to deliver the same amount of heat. Because oil and coal burners for home use tend to be dirtier and less efficient than gas burners, the choice is not as obvious where gas is not available.

An even better solution is electric heating with a heat pump, which is much more efficient overall than resistive heating. A heat pump is just what the name implies. A refrigerator uses a heat pump to extract heat from the low temperature contents of the refrigerator and dump it into the higher temperature surroundings. (Without the pump, of course, heat would flow in the opposite direction.) A heat pump can be used to heat a house simply by making it "refrigerate" the out-of-doors, discharging the heat inside. In summer, the same device can be made to work in reverse as an air conditioner, pumping heat from inside to outside. Under typical operating conditions, a good heat pump can move three units of heat energy—in either direction—for each unit of electrical energy expended. This efficiency, which is three times that of resistive heating, almost exactly compensates for the inefficiency with which electricity is generated. The theoretical efficiency of a heat pump is much higher still; improved designs will undoubtedly be developed to exploit this potential. The initial installation cost of a heat pump is higher than for resistive heating, but this is largely offset by using the pump as an air conditioner as well. In any case, the reduction in electricity consumption through the use of a heat pump is so great that it might be reasonable to ban resistive heating altogether in new construction.

Transportation. America's love affair with the automobile is the single greatest extravagance in the energy budget. Almost 16 percent of the energy consumed annually in the United States feeds the internal combustion engines of passenger cars, and another 2 percent is consumed manufacturing these vehicles.* Yet the automobile is one of the least efficient forms of transportation, averaging only thirty-two

---

*Includes energy consumption needed to produce the steel, rubber, aluminum, etc., that go into automobiles.

passenger miles per gallon of fuel (pmg). Much automobile driving consists of commuting and errand-running with only the driver in the car. Vast savings in energy could be achieved by more sensible transportation, such as greater use of car pools, buses (100-125 pmg), trains (80-200 pmg), bicycles, and walking. The average urban household could save 10,000 kwht annually by replacing two-thirds of its automobile trips of less than two miles with walking or bicycling.* Unfortunately, the mode of transportation whose use is increasing most rapidly with time—the aircraft—is even less efficient than the automobile. A Boeing 707 averages about 21 pmg. Fuel consumption by aircraft could exceed that by passenger cars before 1985.

Not even the advent of a successful electric automobile would greatly alleviate the energy drain of personal transportation. The electricity to power such vehicles would have to be generated at central power plants, many more of which would be required if the switch to electric vehicles were widespread. Overall, electric cars would not be particularly efficient: losses in the motor and control system would probably amount to 10 percent, in charging 20 percent, in transmission and distribution of the electricity 10 percent, and, barring dramatic changes in technology, losses in the generation process would run from 60 to 70 percent. The overall efficiency of the electric car, then, would be 22 to 25 percent, only marginally higher than that of the internal combustion engine *(Bulletin of the Atomic Scientists).*

Shipment of freight is another mode of transportation in which considerable amounts of energy are being squandered. A freight train gets from two to five times as many cargo ton-miles per gallon of fuel as does a truck, yet the percentage of intercity freight carried by trucks is increasing. The rapid increase in air freight is particularly dismaying, inasmuch as this mode of transportation is six times less efficient than even trucking. Clearly, one of the most sensible steps

---

*This calculation and the passenger-mile figures by Prof. Richard A. Rice, in a paper presented at the 1970 Winter Meeting of the American Society of Mechanical Engineers.

that could be taken to reduce energy consumption would be to encourage the use of railroads for both passenger travel and freight. Perhaps if energy becomes expensive enough the market will beat a path to the railroads' door.

Materials and Recycling. A substantial part of the consumption of energy in general and electricity in particular is consumed in the extraction and processing of metals, paper and glass. Estimates of the current role of these materials in the electricity and total energy budgets are given in Figure 12. Among them they account for more than 10 percent of U.S. energy use and almost 15 percent of electricity use. All of these materials are recyclable, yet today only a small fraction of consumption comes from recycling. Usually, recycling uses less energy per pound of product than obtaining new material by the usual processes. Certain other costs, however, are higher for recycling; otherwise profit-conscious industry would be recycling more and mining, logging and so on less. Therefore a substantial increase in the price of energy would have three desirable effects: First, since materials would become more expensive, waste and planned obsolescence would be discouraged. Second, this change would reduce per capita consumption of energy. Finally, since the cost of recycling would increase proportionately less than the cost of the alternatives, industry would be forced to rely more heavily on recycling of raw materials.

The disproportionate energy consumption associated with the production of aluminum deserves special attention. Five times as much energy is necessary to produce a pound of aluminum as to produce a pound of steel. Thus, for example, even though twice as many cans are made from a pound of aluminum as from a pound of steel, the energy requirement per can is two and a half times greater when aluminum is used. The consumption of aluminum in cans and packaging, which now accounts for about 10 percent of all aluminum use, is doubling every seven years. Surely this massive proliferation of disposable and nondegradable containers is a negative contribution to our standard of living rather than a positive one, exclusive of the waste of energy it represents.

A similar situation is the boom in disposable paper products, from diapers to party dresses and sleeping bags. These applications are scandalously wasteful of both paper and energy. Their existence suggests that trees, as well as energy, are badly underpriced.

A Rational Energy Budget. The list of wasteful uses of energy is much longer than this, but the examples given should be enough to suggest that energy consumption per capita could be substantially reduced without a corresponding reduction in true standard of living. Space heating and transportation alone probably use twice as much energy as is reasonable or necessary, so that making appropriate changes in these sectors could reduce per capita consumption by 15 percent. It is difficult to put numbers on the total waste of energy in the materials and manufacturing industries, in household uses of electricity, and in pouring kilowatt-hours into the night sky through flashing signs, but the rising interest in energy problems will surely lead to studies that provide the figures. They should be taken seriously.

Energy promoters have tried to capitalize on ecological concerns by claiming that vast additional amounts of energy will be needed for pollution control, mass transit, sewage treatment and other worthy projects. In some instances this will be true, but in many cases the most intelligent approaches to these problems will be using less energy and not more. Pollution control that involves recycling or devising new uses for waste products may also lead to overall reductions in energy needs.

Changing demand by means of alterations as fundamental as these will be slow. But mobilizing new sources of energy supply and constructing power plants are slow processes, too. Whittling down needless demand is certainly as practical—and far more sensible—than continuing the unthinking attempt to expand supply indefinitely.

Implementing Changes

Some of the changes in demand advocated here will come about automatically, for rises in fuel costs and even minimal pollution control measures will force up the price of energy. As the need to reduce the environmental impact of energy use is taken seriously, energy prices will rise even faster and accelerate the demise of wasteful uses. Some economists have argued that energy demand is "inelastic," that is, that price will have to increase a lot before demand decreases a little. This proposition may be true for residential and personal transportation uses on a short time scale (before people notice what has happened to their gasoline and electricity bills), but business and industry watch their balance sheets more closely. Particularly in the raw materials industries, a rise in energy prices would have immediate substantial effects.

A serious result of increased energy prices is the effect on the poor, for whom the cost of energy is a larger fraction of total expenditures than for most of us. One way to alleviate this problem would be to reverse the existing electricity rate structure. As it stands, large commercial and industrial users get a cheaper rate than home owners, and, across the board, the rate per kwhe goes down as the amount used goes up. Reversing the rate structure would mean that the small user gets the cheapest rate, and that electricity gets more expensive per kwhe as consumption increases. Clearly, this change would encourage responsible use of electricity, and would permit an increase in the average cost of electricity with minimal increase to the poor. Of course, the prices of some products would go up, as intended, so that other measures would be necessary to buffer the impact on the poor. There is no doubt that this country is rich enough to manage this problem. Moreover, steps to improve the lot of the economically disadvantaged are a necessity regardless of what happens to the cost of energy.

Another misguided practice is the use of low rates to encourage consumption during off-peak hours. The idea here is to increase the utilization factor of generating plants by reducing the difference in demand that exists between peak and off-peak periods of electricity use. This method, of course, tends to reduce the difference by making demand high all the time. It apparently has not occurred to the utilities that the utilization factor of existing plants can be raised (and the need for new plants diminished) if the difference in demand is reduced by making demand *small* all the time. In other words, why not impose a surcharge on using electricity during periods of peak demand?

Demand for electricity could also be reduced by outlawing promotional advertising by utilities. (Consolidated Edison of New York has already quit voluntarily.) This approach could not interfere with meeting genuine needs for electricity because it is not necessary to advertise to tell people what their needs are. In supporting the "right" to manufacture demand through advertising, while claiming at the same time that "for the next three decades, we will be in a race for our lives to meet our energy needs,"* the utilities and their spokesmen on government regulatory bodies insult the intelligence of the public.

Prerequisite to virtually all the needed changes is a change in the mandate of the Federal Power Commission, the body charged in the Federal Power Act with "assuring an abundant supply of electric energy throughout the United States with the greatest possible economy and with regard to the proper utilization and conservation of natural resources." The FPC has made clear by its behavior that it considers regard for natural resources to be the least of its concerns. But it is now time for cheap and abundant energy to take a back seat to the needs of maintaining a livable environment. Such new priorities will be implemented only by the force of law.

Energy and the Poor Countries

Today, the United States and other rich regions (Canada, the U.S.S.R., Japan, Europe and Oceania) account for about 85 percent of the world's annual energy consumption, while the poor countries—comprising more than two-thirds of the world's population—account for only 15 per cent.

---

*Federal Power Commissioner John A. Carver, Jr., quoted in *The Economy, Energy, and the Environment.*

Improving the standard of living in the poor countries will call for large increases in their energy consumption, and it would be preposterous for the rest of us to claim now that the poor countries should stabilize their energy consumption for environmental reasons. The cost of minimizing the local environmental impact of new energy sources in the poor countries is something we should expect to help them with. In terms of the global impact of energy consumption, including carbon dioxide and particulate matter in the atmosphere and oil in the oceans, it is the rich countries that have already taxed the capacity of the environment to absorb abuse, and it is we who must cut back to permit the attainment of a decent standard of living elsewhere.

Nevertheless, it should not be assumed that energy alone will bring about prosperity. It is a necessary but not sufficient ingredient, and the fraction of the *cost* of development represented by energy is not large. For example, electricity is of no value without the light bulbs, appliances and industries that consume it, and the cost of these far exceeds the cost of the energy they use. This fact suggests that the cost of energy is not the limiting factor in development today, and that it would not be the limiting factor even if necessary pollution control made energy considerably more expensive. Actually, raising the standard of living in the poor countries at any meaningful rate will be a gargantuan task whether energy is particularly cheap or not. *(Population/Resources/ Environment)*. Real progress will require the diversion of energy and raw materials from frivolous uses in the rich countries to necessity-oriented uses in the poor ones.

Unfortunately, the legitimate needs of the poor both at home and abroad have often been used as a blanket justification for more of the same kinds of economic and technological growth that have helped to create today's predicament. Those who use this ploy are really saying that the only route for world-wide prosperity is the escalation of today's wasteful technologies to even higher plateaus of profligacy. In other words, we will not be able to give the poor many crumbs until our own loaf, already more than ample, gets even bigger. This proposition assumes, of course, that the present inequitable distribution of the fruits of technology will persist. Such a future is neither necessary nor desirable. We can work for a better one.

8. Conclusions

No easy answers were promised here, and none have been forthcoming. Questions concerning the relative merits of alternative energy sources, the desirability of various patterns of consumption, and the precise economic repercussions of changes in prices and regulation need much more study before definitive statements will be possible. These questions are at the heart of what may come to be called The Great Energy Debate, in which the conflict between energy's central role in environmental degradation and its necessity for material prosperity must ultimately be resolved. The debate is just beginning, and this book is an attempt to arm the concerned citizen with some of the tools needed to follow and participate in it. The main themes that have been developed here can be rather concisely summarized:

1. The fossil fuels that supply most energy today, and the uranium-235 that fuels existing nuclear reactors, are finite in supply but not in immediate danger of being exhausted. Questions of public health, environmental deterioration, and exploiting the cheap energy resources of the poor countries are more important in the short term than resource exhaustion.

2. Problems of electricity demand and the proliferation of power plants cannot be considered in isolation from the rest of the energy crisis. Electricity is only one form of energy consumption; often it can replace or be replaced by other forms.

3. No means of providing energy, electrical or otherwise, is entirely free of environmental liabilities, and no form of pollution control is 100 percent effective. Thus, there will always be some environmental impact associated with energy production.

4. All uses of energy produce heat. If every other environmental cost of energy consumption could be held to tolerable levels, this one would eventually force a halt to growth.

5. In general, a crisis in supply and demand can be met by increasing supply *or* by stabilizing demand. Energy promoters have been unwilling to consider the second possibility, but they have failed to show why not.

6. Much energy is now being wasted. Per capita consumption can be greatly reduced without crippling the economy or the standard of living.

7. Our preoccupation with the cheapness of energy no longer serves us well. Bringing environmental costs into the balance sheets will raise the price of energy, which will have many beneficial effects. Policies to counter the adverse effect on the poor are necessary and attainable.

8. Rising costs of energy, and other policies to stabilize per capita demand, will ultimately be of no avail if the number of consumers increases without limit. After a point, population growth requires a disproportionate increase in energy consumption just to keep per capita affluence constant, because of diminishing returns.

The energy promoters are caught in a trap of their own making. Owing to failures of foresight (*not* lack of resources in the ground), they will probably be unable to meet energy demand on the scale they believe is desirable and necessary during the next decade. These failures include fixing the price of natural gas at an unrealistically low level for many years; insufficient attention to gasification and liquefaction of coal and the development of oil shales; underestimation of public concern with environmental quality; shortages of tankers, coal cars, and miners; and many others. The environmentalists should, in a sense, be thankful for these planning failures, for they seem likely to slow down the rate of growth of energy consumption even if sane analysis does not. Technology simply does not respond fast enough to rescue the energy promoters overnight—power plants, pipelines, coal mines, and oil fields all take years between drawing board and production, even without public opposition. Where technology cannot respond, of course, the projected consumption will suffer. If this does not happen by means of conscious decisions concerning what forms of consumption are expendable, brownouts and blackouts will help make the choices for us.

We need not simply sit back and watch, however. To leave energy planning stumbling along in the current disarray would be to invite mistakes more serious than those that have already occurred. With due regard for the complexities of energy problems and the questions that remain unanswered, we know enough to take *some* sensible steps today. The following list of proposals for action, based on arguments presented in the foregoing chapters, is a beginning.

1. Support stiffer fines for oil spills and tighter regulations on emissions from fossil fuel power plants.

2. Oppose the deployment of breeder reactors and the rapid proliferation of conventional fission reactors until questions of safety, insurance, radioactive waste disposal, independent setting and enforcement of standards, and control of bomb-grade material are satisfactorily resolved.

3. Demand legislation requiring that all land that has been strip mined be reclaimed, that uranium mine tailings and acid drainage from coal wastes be controlled, and that additional measures to protect the health of coal and uranium miners be implemented.

4. Urge that the promotional rate structure for electricity

be reversed and that advertising by utilities be prohibited.

5. Urge that the Federal Power Act be amended to give first priority to minimizing environmental impact of generating electricity, and to permit the FPC to investigate ways to diminish demand.

6. Support greatly increased federal support for research on techniques that promise to minimize the environmental impact of energy production and/or increase the efficiency of conversion to electricity—including solar energy, controlled fusion, MHD and fuel cells.

7. Lobby for a comprehensive national energy policy, incorporating all energy sources and continuously reevaluating options for the short and long term.

8. Reduce your own energy consumption: drive a small car, form a car pool, take the train, ride a bike, add insulation to your home, ask for a heat pump in your next one, encourage recycling.

9. Use the savings to join the Sierra Club, Friends of the Earth and Zero Population Growth. And keep informed.

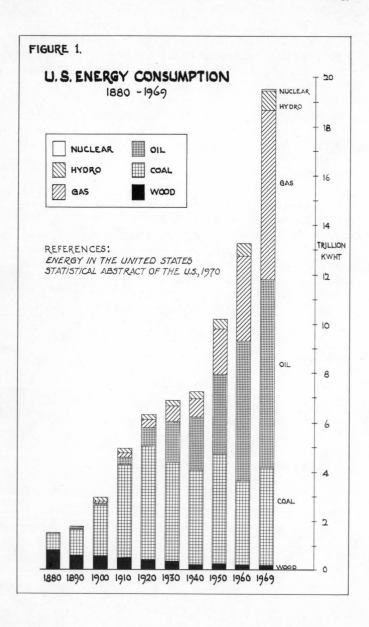

FIGURE 1.

U.S. ENERGY CONSUMPTION
1880 - 1969

FIGURE 2.

DEPLETION OF FOSSIL FUELS

NOTE: SUPPLY FOR ALL FUELS HAS BEEN CONVERTED FROM THE USUAL UNITS (CUBIC FEET, BARRELS, METRIC TONS) TO TRILLION KWHT

	INITIAL SUPPLY (TRILLION KWHT)	Yp* (DATE, A.D.)	Y90• (DATE, A.D.)
NATURAL GAS (U.S. LESS ALASKA)	407	1980	2015
CRUDE OIL (U.S. LESS ALASKA)	275	1970	2000
CRUDE OIL (WORLD)	2,240	1990	2020
COAL (U.S.)	5,920	2175	2400
COAL (WORLD)	34,400	2110	2700

* Yp = YEAR OF PEAK CONSUMPTION.
• Y90 = YEAR IN WHICH 90% OF TOTAL CUMULATIVE CONSUMPTION IS BEHIND US.
SOURCE: CONDENSED AND ADAPTED FROM M. KING HUBBERT, IN *RESOURCES & MAN*.

FIGURE 3. SOURCES OF AIR POLLUTION IN THE U.S. 1968

(PERCENTAGES BY WEIGHT)

SOURCE	CARBON MONOXIDE (100 MILLION TONS)	SULFUR OXIDES (33 MILLION TONS)	HYDROCARBONS (32 MILLION TONS)	NITROGEN OXIDES (21 MILLION TONS)	PARTICULATES (28 MILLION TONS)
FUEL BURNING FOR TRANSPORTATION	63.8%	2.4%	51.9%	39.3%	4.3%
FUEL BURNING IN STATIONARY SOURCES	1.9	73.5	2.2	48.5	31.4
INDUSTRIAL PROCESSES OTHER THAN FUEL BURNING	9.6	22.0	14.4	1.0	26.5
SOLID WASTE DISPOSAL	7.8	0.3	5.0	2.9	3.9
MISCELLANEOUS *	16.9	1.8	26.5	8.3	33.9

* INCLUDES FOREST FIRES, AGRICULTURAL BURNING, COAL WASTE FIRES, GASOLINE MARKETING.

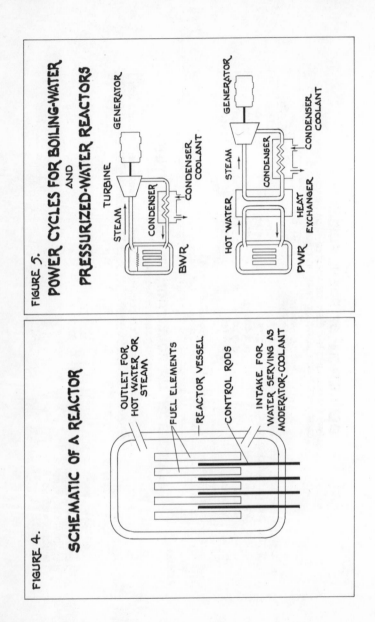

FIGURE 5.

POWER CYCLES FOR BOILING-WATER
AND
PRESSURIZED-WATER REACTORS

FIGURE 4.

SCHEMATIC OF A REACTOR

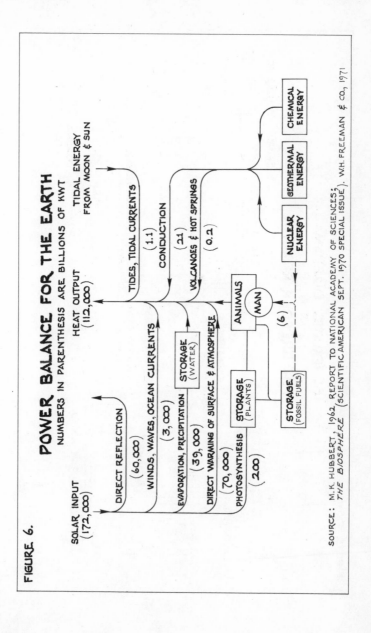

FIGURE 6.

POWER BALANCE FOR THE EARTH

NUMBERS IN PARENTHESIS ARE BILLIONS OF KWT

SOLAR INPUT (172,000)

HEAT OUTPUT (112,000)

TIDAL ENERGY FROM MOON & SUN

DIRECT REFLECTION (60,000)

WINDS, WAVES, OCEAN CURRENTS (3,000)

EVAPORATION, PRECIPITATION (39,000)

DIRECT WARMING OF SURFACE & ATMOSPHERE (70,000)

PHOTOSYNTHESIS (200)

STORAGE (WATER)

STORAGE (PLANTS)

STORAGE (FOSSIL FUELS)

ANIMALS

MAN (6)

TIDES, TIDAL CURRENTS (1.1)

CONDUCTION (21)

VOLCANOS & HOT SPRINGS (0.2)

NUCLEAR ENERGY

GEOTHERMAL ENERGY

CHEMICAL ENERGY

SOURCE: M.K. HUBBERT, 1962, REPORT TO NATIONAL ACADEMY OF SCIENCES; *THE BIOSPHERE* (SCIENTIFIC AMERICAN SEPT. 1970 SPECIAL ISSUE). W.H. FREEMAN & CO., 1971

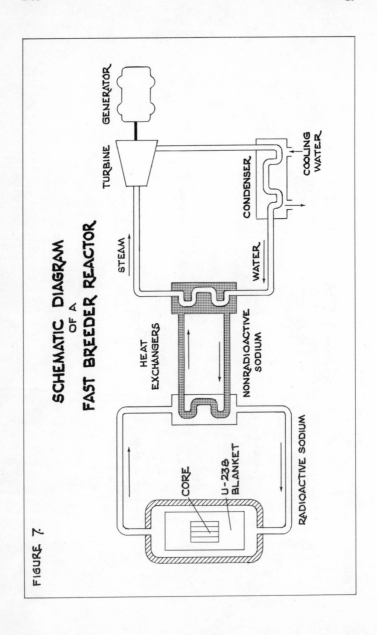

FIGURE 7

SCHEMATIC DIAGRAM OF A FAST BREEDER REACTOR

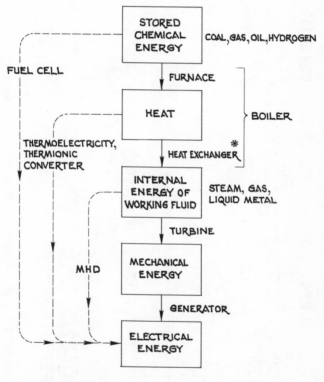

FIGURE 8.

ENERGY CONVERSION WITH CHEMICAL FUELS

*NONE REQUIRED IF COMBUSTION GASES SERVE AS WORKING FLUID

FIGURE 9.   ENERGY, ELECTRICITY, AND PROSPERITY

COUNTRY	GNP PER CAPITA (U.S. DOLLARS)	ANNUAL ENERGY CONSUMPTION PER CAPITA (KWHT)	RATIO OF KWHT TO DOLLARS	ANNUAL ELECTRICITY CONSUMPTION PER CAPITA (KWHE)
SWITZERLAND	2,754	24,000	8.7	4,026
NEW ZEALAND	2,000	21,500	10.7	4,297
JAPAN	1,404	20,000	14.3	2,377
NORWAY	2,362	34,000	14.4	13,566
U.S.A.	4,379	82,500	18.9	6,612
CANADA	2,997	68,000	22.6	8,111
U.S.S.R.	970	32,500	35.0	2,487

SOURCE: UNITED NATIONS STATISTICAL YEARBOOK, 1969, U.N., NEW YORK

FIGURE 10.   BREAKDOWN OF ENERGY AND ELECTRICITY CONSUMPTION (U.S., 1968)

ALL ENERGY SOURCES

ELECTRIC GENERATION FOR ALL PURPOSES	22.5%
NON-ELECTRIC HOUSEHOLD & COMMERCIAL	21.8%
NON-ELECTRIC TRANSPORTATION	24.2%
NON-ELECTRIC INDUSTRIAL	31.0%
OTHER	0.5%

ELECTRIC COMPONENT

HOUSEHOLD	32%
COMMERCIAL	21%
INDUSTRIAL	43%
OTHER	4%

SOURCE: STATISTICAL ABSTRACT OF THE UNITED STATES, 1970 EDITION

FIGURE 11.

SELECTED USES OF ENERGY IN THE U.S. IN 1960

INCLUDES ELECTRIC & NON-ELECTRIC CONSUMPTION

	PERCENT OF CATEGORY	PERCENT OF TOTAL
INDUSTRIAL		35.2%
GENERAL MANUFACTURING	47.0%	16.5
IRON & STEEL	20.0	7.0
PETROLEUM REFINING	10.0	3.5
TRANSPORTATION		20.3
AUTOMOBILES	56.5	11.5
TRUCKS	21.8	4.4
RESIDENTIAL		19.8
SPACE HEATING	58.0	11.5
WATER HEATING	12.7	2.5
LIGHTING	5.9	1.2
COMMERCIAL & OTHER		24.7
COMMERCIAL	35.0	8.6
DEFENSE	10.2	2.5
AGRICULTURE	8.0	2.0

SOURCE: *RESOURCES IN AMERICA'S FUTURE*

FIGURE 12.

ENERGY CONSUMPTION IN PROVIDING BASIC MATERIALS, U.S. 1968

	FRACTION OF TOTAL ENERGY USE *	FRACTION OF ALL ELECTRICITY USE ●
STEEL	6.0%	2.5%
ALUMINUM	1.5	4.0
OTHER METALS	1.0	1.5
PAPER	1.8	4.0
GLASS	0.3	1.5

* COURTESY MR. ARJUN MAKHIJANI, DEPARTMENT OF ELECTRICAL ENGINEERING, UNIVERSITY OF CALIFORNIA AT BERKELEY.

● ESTIMATED FROM PROJECTIONS IN *RESOURCES IN AMERICA'S FUTURE*.

ACKNOWLEDGMENT

Thanks are due to Dr. Paul Ehrlich, Mrs. Jane Bavelas and my wife Cheri for helpful comments on the manuscript, and to Mr. Arjun Makhijani for making available his figures on energy consumption in the materials and automotive industries.

REFERENCES CITED

(alphabetically, by title for books and reports, by name of journal for articles)

The Biosphere, W. H. Freeman and Co. (San Francisco) 1970.

Bulletin of the Atomic Scientists, p. 29 (May 1970) "The Economic Impact of Electric Vehicles—a Scenario," Bruce C. Netschert.

The Careless Atom, Sheldon Novick, Houghton Mifflin (Boston) 1969; paperback edition, Dell (New York).

Cleaning Our Environment: The Chemical Basis for Action, American Chemical Society (Washington, D.C.) 1969.

Direct Use of the Sun's Energy, Farrington Daniels, Yale University Press (New Haven) 1964.

The Economy, Energy, and the Environment, Joint Committee Print, 91st Congress, 2nd Session, U.S. Government Printing Office (Washington, D.C.) Sept. 1, 1970.

Energy in the United States, Hans H. Landsberg and Sam H. Schurr, Random House (New York) 1968.

"Energy Resources," M. King Hubbert, in *Resources and Man,* Committee on Resources and Man of the National Academy of Sciences, W. H. Freeman and Co., (San Francisco) 1969.

Environmental Cost of Electric Power, Dean E. Abrahamson, Scientists' Institute for Public Information (New York), 1970.

Environmental Effects of Producing Electric Power, Hearings of the Joint Committee on Atomic Energy, Part I (1 vol.) and Part II (2 vols.), U.S. Government Printing Office (Washington, D.C.) 1969 and 1970.

Environmental Quality (First Annual Report of the Council on Environmental Quality), U.S. Government Printing Office (Washington, D.C.) 1970.

Global Ecology: Readings toward a Rational Strategy for Man, J. P. Holdren and P. R. Ehrlich, editors, Harcourt Brace Jovanovich (New York) 1971.

Lectures on Physics, Richard P. Feynman, Robert B. Leighton, and Matthew Sands, Addison-Wesley (Reading, Massachusetts) 1963.

Man's Impact on the Global Environment (Study of Critical Environmental Problems), M.I.T. Press (Cambridge, Mass.) 1970.

Oil on Ice, Tom Brown, Sierra Club Books (New York) 1971.

Nuclear Safety, Vol. 11, p. 283 (July-August 1970) "Safety Assessment of Fast Sodium-Cooled Reactors in the United Kingdom," F. R. Farmer.

Poisoned Power, John W. Gofman and Arthur R. Tamplin, Rodale Press, (Emmaus, Pa.) 1971.

Population/Resources/Environment, Paul R. Ehrlich and Anne H. Ehrlich, W. H. Freeman and Co. (San Francisco) 1970.

Power for the People, Aden B. Meinel and Marjorie P. Meinel, to be published.

Resources in America's Future. Hans H. Landsberg, Leonard L. Fischman, and Joseph L. Fisher, Johns Hopkins Press for Resources for the Future (Baltimore) 1963.

Science, Vol. 162, p. 857 (22 Nov. 1968) "Power from the Sun: Its Future," Peter E. Glaser.

Science, Vol. 169, p. 821 (28 Aug. 1970) "Clean Power from Coal," A. M. Squires.

Science, Vol. 172, p. 143 (9 April 1971) "Plutonium: Reactor Proliferation Threatens a Black Market," Deborah Shapely.

Science, Vol. 172, p. 660 (14 May 1971) "Solar Energy: A Feasible Source of Power?", Allen L. Hammond.

Science, Vol. 172, p. 918 (28 May 1971) "Nuclear Reactor Safety: A Skeleton at the Feast?", Robert Gillette.

Scientific American, Feb. 1971, p. 50, "The Prospects of Fusion Power," William C. Gough and Bernard J. Eastlund.

Scientific American, May 1971, p. 70, "Cooling Towers," Riley D. Woodson.

Statistical Abstract of the U.S., 1970, Department of Commerce, U.S. Government Printing Office (Washington, D.C.) 1970.

WASH-740, "Theoretical Possibilities and Consequences of Major Accidents in Large Power Plants," U.S. Atomic Energy Commission, 1957.

OTHER REFERENCES

The Challenge of Man's Future, Harrison Brown, Viking (New York), 1954. Contains readable, informative treatment of the history of energy, and its central role in present and possible future industrial societies.

Global Effects of Environmental Pollution, S. F. Singer, editor, Springer-Verlag (New York) 1970. For readers with strong technical background, this book surveys recent knowledge on gaseous pollutants and their effects on climate.

"Impact of Population Growth," P. R. Ehrlich and J. P. Holdren, *Science*, Vol. 171, p. 1212 (26 March 1971). Gives more details of relation between population growth and consumption and pollution.

Man and the Ecosphere, P. R. Ehrlich, J. P. Holdren, and R. W. Holm, editors, W. H. Freeman and Co. (San Francisco) 1971. Includes basic *Scientific American* articles on flow of energy, resources and pollutants through the biosphere.

"Population and Panaceas: A Technological Perspective," P. R. Ehrlich and J. P. Holdren, *BioScience*, Vol. 19, p. 1065 (Dec. 1969). Discusses potential and limitations of technology, including new energy sources, in coping with needs of growing populations, with emphasis on underdeveloped countries.

Selected Materials on Environmental Effects of Producing Electric Power, Joint Committee on Atomic Energy, U.S. Government Printing Office (Washington, D.C.) August 1969.

U.S. Energy Policies: An Agenda for Research, Resources for the Future Staff Report, Johns Hopkins Press (Baltimore) 1968. Contains much information on regulatory policies and other aspects of government involvement in energy industries.

Part two

Power:
conflicts and
resolutions

by Philip Herrera

AUTHOR'S NOTE

The following chapters describe some of the major recent controversies over the siting and operation of power plants. Each controversy represents the clash between two distinct definitions of the public interest. On one side is the insatiable demand of Americans for more and more electricity, on the other a deep and growing concern for the American environment and a desire by private citizens to participate in the public decisions that affect environment.

The citizens of America are justifiably concerned. Their complaint against power development starts with the extraction of fuel from the earth. In quest of coal, brute machines have ripped up thousands of square miles of the United States, leaving them sterile and desolate, rust-colored mine acids slowly seeping through the scarred land to poison nearby waterways. Oil's record is scarcely better. A ruptured oil dome caused a massive gooey mess in the Santa Barbara Channel, and a defective well polluted miles of the Gulf of Mexico off Louisiana in 1970. That year, too, 4,000 oil spills were reported to the Coast Guard: an estimated 3,500 others went unreported, though the oil itself lingered on and on in the waters.

Getting power to the people also gobbles up land. Coal-fired electric plants use vast acreage for coal storage yards and railroad facilities to receive and switch 100-car-long trains. Nuclear plants need open space as a safety buffer to insulate themselves from people. Then there are transmission lines. Right now 300,000 miles of these lines weave across 4 million acres of the landscape. By 1990, another 200,000 miles will be needed, occupying another 3.1 million acres, or twice the area of Delaware. Where will it end? The Committee on Environmental Information has gone to the trouble of establishing one absolute limit. If demand for electricity continues to double every decade and if each power plant were only 1,000 feet to a side, in 185 years the entire surface of the United States would be covered by generating stations leaving no room for houses, farms, factories—or even transmission lines.

1. The Dilemmas of Power

Case study:
The Four Corners.

Almost everyone loves electricity—and hates power plants. Especially fossil fuel plants. Ugly, dirty, smelly and noisy, they shroud their surroundings in a man-made miasma of soot and noxious gases. And nobody wants one in his backyard. Dislike leads to dispute; individuals band together to fight off the stinkers, or entire smoggy cities—the consumption centers of power—ban additional plants because they foul already polluted air beyond safe limits. The final step in the process is sharply ironic: because demand for energy never wanes, new generating stations are sited in places where the air is still clean and thus can legally accept the ambient filth. The juice crackles to market on long, unsightly transmission lines. And pollution spreads, as it were, by popular demand.

This familiar sequence of events is certainly sad and probably morally obscene as well. There are no empty backyards in the United States any longer. Somebody always suffers, especially if he does not want the benefit of more electricity himself. This is also one of the many dilemmas of power — trade-offs are routinely made at the expense of the communal environment. (If everybody owns the environment, then it belongs to nobody, right?) But example is better than precept. Heed now the history of Black Mesa and Four Corners, which even utility executives who make the hard decisions now call "the school of horrors."

In the mid-1950s a group of the Southwest's major electric utilities, recognizing their region's phenomenal growth, started searching for a good spot to put power plants that would provide energy for the burgeoning cities, especially Los Angeles, Phoenix and Las Vegas. Since nuclear stations were still much too small and experimental to figure in these plans, the companies were concerned with fossil-fired facilities. What the utilities needed, then, was a place with adequate supplies of fuel and water. As for air pollution — a growing problem even then — they decided to go someplace where no one lived and, presumably, no one would complain.

The search ended successfully, as it were, in the wide open desert area where New Mexico, Arizona, Utah and Colorado all meet — at the "Four Corners." There were thick, untouched seams of coal lying close to the surface in the vicinity and, though water was scarce, the Colorado River and its tributaries could just slake the power plants' thirst. Moreover, the population was sparse and poor, mostly Navajo and Hopi Indians. These people, the utilities believed, would eagerly welcome economic development of their lands and the good things money would bring.

The utilities formed a consortium known as Western Energy Supply and Transmission (WEST) consisting of twenty-three public and investor-owned companies. Together, they planned what would be the U.S.'s biggest power complex to produce approximately 36,000 megawatts of electricity in the 1980s—more than twice the Tennessee Valley Authority's total. The heart of the complex would comprise six enormous plants in four states. Two of the monsters—Four Corners (2,075 megawatts) and San Juan (990 megawatts)—would be sited a few miles apart on the San Juan River near Farmington, New Mexico. Two others—Navajo (2,310 megawatts) and Kaiparowits (5,000 megawatts,

minimum)—would stand on opposite sides of the man-made
Lake Powell, one in Arizona and the other in Utah. The
Mohave plant (2,310 megawatts) would be in nearby
Nevada, downstream from Lake Powell on the Colorado
River. The sixth, Huntington Canyon (2,000 megawatts),
would be in central Utah on Huntington Creek.

To be sure, there was no dearth of legal problems
standing in the way of implementing such an ambitious
scheme. For one, much of the land and the coal under it
belonged to the Indians. For another, the U.S. Department
of the Interior and other federal agencies would have to
approve road building, tapping the already overdroughted
Colorado River Basin and stringing transmission lines
through federally owned land. But those problems were
surmountable. The states themselves actively wanted these
additions to their tax bases. Representatives of the tribes,
urged on by the U.S. Bureau of Indian Affairs, struck what
sounded like advantageous deals with coal companies. The
Interior Department contracted to supply cooling water to
the coal companies at the surprisingly low price of seven
dollars per acre-foot (according to one informed estimate,
the "going" price to other users was twenty-eight dollars
an acre-foot). Later on, Interior was to participate in the
Navajo plant because it needed abundant power to pump
water to central Arizona.

All these schemes and negotiations were carried out not
exactly in a news blackout but as quietly and unobtrusively
as possible. Correspondence between various federal agencies
in 1969 reveals that most government employees did not
even know for sure of the existence of the Navajo plant until
months after Interior Secretary Stewart Udall had signed a
water service contract with Navajo's operator, the Salt River
Project. Meantime there had been no public hearings, no
congressional hearings, no announcements. While such
pervasive silence now raises troubling questions of just whom
the federal agencies were representing—the people or the
power consortium—at the time, it speeded implementation
of the various aspects of the project.

Four Corners, the first plant to go into operation in 1963, soon shocked environmentalists into an awareness of the power complex and its potential consequences. Operated by Arizona Public Service, the plant turned out to be a tremendous polluter, perhaps the worst single one in the nation. Burning coal from a nearby strip mine operated by Utah Mining & Construction Company, it daily chuffed into the air 300 tons of particulate matter—more than is permitted in New York City and Los Angeles combined—plus huge quantities of dangerous sulfur dioxide and nitrogen oxide pollutants. So dirty was the plume that it has been tracked by private plane for 215 miles over the West. While in the atmosphere, this ambient filth interfered with the view from major observatories that had expressly chosen to locate in the desert because of the pellucid air. When the soot eventually fell back to earth, it landed on the area's six national parks, three national recreation areas and twenty-eight national monuments. Investigation later revealed a partial cause of the trouble. The plant's operator had not bothered to install two-thirds of the pollution abatement devices specified in its contract. Belatedly, New Mexico ordered the plant to clean up by the end of 1971 or shut down.

The only other plant yet to start operations was Mohave, in 1970. Unlike Four Corners, it was fully equipped from the start with electrostatic precipitators to capture 97 percent of sooty emissions. But in the eyes of many observers, this plant has a different kind of flaw. Its coal comes from a strip mine on the Indian reservation, not just out in some unpopulated wild but at Black Mesa. This 3,300-square-mile plateau has been described by William Brown, a former environmental specialist with the National Park Service, as "an island of forest and grass in the desert, last outpost of ancient cultures." Its southern part has been the home of the Hopi for centuries; in the north, where the mesa reaches 8,000 feet, the Navajo garden and raise cattle and sheep.

Over time both tribes have developed a land ethic of

stewardship, not of rapacity. To the many "traditionalists" among the Indians, the mesa with its solitude and haunting beauty is sacred, the center of the universe. They regard what white people call Mother Nature as everything that is important—church, shrine, heritage and legacy all combined. Thus they see the mammoth power shovels and draglines of the Peabody Coal Company cruelly injuring the body of the Earth Mother, and they are aghast. "It is prophesied that the Indians will have their lands confiscated or ruined by force and by lies," warns David Monongye, traditionalist leader of the Hopi village of Hotevilla. "It is prophesied that if the Hopi and their friends cannot stop this, the world will end. It will turn over. And none will survive, none."

Between 1960 and 1966 "progressive"—i.e., development-minded—tribesmen leased mineral rights to Peabody Coal on 64,858 acres of Black Mesa. The company expects to mine 13 million tons of coal during the next thirty-five years, grubbing through about 400 acres a year to supply the Mohave plant with 16,000 tons of coal a day and the Navajo plant (when it goes on line in 1974) with a daily quota of 23,000 tons. In return for the coal, Peabody is paying the Indians an average of $3 million in annual royalties for those thirty-five years and has promised to hire tribesmen whenever it can. Another promise is to regrade the land to its original contours and then to replant native vegetation on the disturbed earth. Critics doubt whether such reclamation is in fact possible. So far, only tumbleweed has grown on the spoil banks, though other varieties of grasses may eventually take hold. The coal company, for its part, will gross about $750 million for its work on Black Mesa during the next thirty-five years.

As if to add to the desecration of Black Mesa by strip mining, the "progressive" tribesmen also entered into another, potentially even more damaging arrangement with Peabody. After the coal has been ripped from the ground, it is pulverized and sent in a half-water, half-coal slurry to the Mohave plant through an underground pipeline 275 miles long. The water, by far the most precious commodity in the arid Southwest, comes from wells driven 2,000 or more feet deep in the leased land. At that depth are water-bearing geologic formations, or aquifers, which Peabody says are "completely separated" from the shallow water supplies used by the Indians. In a further attempt not to deplete the tribes' water reserves, the company has lined its wells with concrete casing so that ground water will not seep into them. There is nevertheless no conclusive evidence indicating just what will happen after Peabody has tapped the aquifers for some time. All the Indians know is that the pipeline operating at capacity requires 4,500 gallons of water per minute, or 3,200 acre-feet a year (for which Peabody is paying rates ranging from $1.67 to $5.00 an acre-foot). That is a great deal of water in an already dessicated land. Mina Lansa, woman chief of the Hopi settlement of Old Oraibi, puts her peoples' plight simply: "What is money? It comes quickly and is quickly spent. But the land is there forever. If it is torn up and the water is taken, we will starve."

To stop the despoliation, the traditionalists (who form a majority of the tribes) argue that all the leases with Peabody Coal Company are illegal. True, they were signed by the progressive tribal council, with the approval of the Bureau of Indian Affairs. But the Indians' constitutions also provide that any representative on the tribal council must also be approved by his village chiefs, which was often not done. Hence, the leases may not be valid, a slim possibility that would seriously delay the consortium's plans.

The consortium has had to face unwelcome surprises from other sources. Many major conservation groups, including the Environmental Defense Fund, National Wildlife Federation and Sierra Club plus the Native American Rights Fund, have brought court action against the involved federal agencies. One suit, for example, charges that the agencies failed to issue environmental "impact" statements (now required) on the effects of various water withdrawal permits and grants of right-of-way. While such actions have been brought too late to affect the two completed plants or the three others now under construction, they may at least postpone Kaiparowits, the biggest of the lot. Another court action contends that each of the plants must be licensed by the Federal Power Commission because they take great gulps from the Colorado River Basin.

Like stones thrown into a stagnant pool, efforts by such local groups as the Central Clearing House and Black Mesa Defense Fund to publicize the environmental effects of the whole complex of plants have rippled out to a horrified public. *Life* magazine ran a story entitled "Hello Energy— Goodbye Big Sky." And in May, 1971, a coalition of conservation groups took full-page ads in *The New York Times, Los Angeles Times* and other newspapers to protest the devastation of the Southwest. The headline— . . . *Like Ripping Apart St. Peter's, In Order to Sell the Marble*— guaranteed attention. Best of all, in May, 1971, the Senate Interior Committee held a week of hearings in the affected states to see if it could help resolve the problems.

It could not. But the hearings did define the dilemmas. In his introductory statement, Senator Henry Jackson described the fundamental conflict. "The situation which we have here is in many respects representative of the complexity and difficulty of the environmental issues facing our nation everywhere. The fact seems undeniable that at least the major part of the energy to be produced by these plants is urgently needed," he said. "On the other hand, it appears certain that the development, regardless of the very best measures which technology can provide, will have some significant environmental impacts. The desert area, until recently, has remained sparsely populated and undeveloped. Its unparalleled scenery and unique ecological systems in vast areas have been undisturbed by the works of man. The development will surely make significant changes in that situation."

Executives of the electric utilities presented their case by emphasizing the benefits of having great blocks of cheap power available. They argued that electricity creates employment, thus causes a higher standard of living. (As *Life* put it, *Hello Energy.*) More electricity is needed, among other things, to save the environment by powering sewage treatment plants, mass transit, junk compressors, recycling processes. (*Hello Survival?*) Moreover, WEST's new plants would be outfitted with the very latest in pollution abatement devices and so would meet all applicable air quality standards.

But the plants are so big, countered many environmentalists, that even if they had the best safeguards, they would still emit 240 tons of fly ash every day, plus 2,160 tons of sulfur dioxide and 1,350 tons of nitrogen oxides. (*Goodbye Big Sky.*) By withdrawing more than 80 billion gallons annually from the Colorado River Basin, the plants would also increase the salinity content of the water flowing downstream to thirsty southwestern farms. (*Goodbye Sweet Water.*) And then there were the virtually permanent ravages of strip mining to consider. (*Goodbye Landscape.*)

Among the 150 witnesses, several suggested solutions. Hear their voices: Richard Morgan, research associate at the Southwest Research and Information Center on the present decision-making system and its reliance on the force of inertia:

> The WEST Regional Advisory Committee claims that the West's power needs will quadruple again by 1990. That means we will need plants like San Juan, Navajo and Kaiparowits. And almost as soon as they are operational, we will need to duplicate them. Our demand will quadruple again by 2010 and again by 2030. The picture that emerges is that of a 2,000-megawatt plant every ten miles; and power poles lined up in every direction as far as the eye can see through a dense smog over endless stretches of Peabody Coal's "reclaimed" land. It is not a pretty picture, but it is not entirely a fantasy. This is the path we are on right now.

Morgan had a specific suggestion:

> We request a moratorium on all power plant development in the Southwest. In the meantime, measures could be instituted to alter rate structures so that they reflect the true environmental costs of using electricity, and to ban all advertising which serves to increase power con-

sumption. These actions could only result in an increase
in the quality of our lives.

Here is Brant Calkin, chairman of the Rio Grande chapter
of the Sierra Club on the federal government's role:

We need a national land use policy. We have based
our traditional attitudes on the idea that land was un-
limited. But no single land area can be everything to all
people, and we have to plan for those uses which may
be mutually exclusive. Previous attitudes defined the
Southwest as a scenic and recreational wonderland. It
should not become the utility backyard of Los Angeles
or Phoenix by default.

We need a national fuel and energy policy. We have
attacked our power needs with all the enthusiasm of
the woodchopper who doesn't have time to sharpen his
axe. We must take the time to define the point of
diminishing returns in energy growth and we must do it
now.

New Mexico's supervisor of air quality control, Dick
Burgard, focused on the electric utilities:

The long-range effects of large, low-grade coal-
fueled plants have not been studied in any depth. With
large quantities of fine particulate matter being emitted,
the questions are being posed as to whether we are
creating problems similar to those which could have
been produced by the SST. We feel that before any
additional power development takes place, it is reasonable for utility industries to do their environmental
homework in advance.

In this search for solutions, one has to remember the
Hopi Indians' Mina Lansa, all of four-feet, seven-inches tall
and indomitable:

We don't want money from the coal companies. We
love all earth and nature. Black Mesa is the heart of
Mother Earth. We get life from earth. We get food.
Money go away fast. Then nothing you have left. We
have no land. Then we have nothing.

2. The Challenge to Industry

Case study:
Commonwealth Edison.

In the eighty-one years since Thomas Edison set up the
first steam electric generating station to serve a portion of
lower Manhattan, the electric power industry has reached
out to serve the nation. Transmission lines today snake to
the remotest villages, and power plants everywhere dot
the map. In terms of capital investment, the electric utilities
form the biggest U.S. industry, accounting for more than
12 percent of all private spending on plants and equipment.
In terms of reliability, the industry's record is almost
incredible. A study by the Edison Electric Institute, an
industry organization of private utilities, shows that in the
decade 1958-1968, the average consumer had electricity
99.98 percent of the time. No wonder the typical American
home contains sixteen electric appliances.

The first blemish on the industry's public face appeared
in the late 1920s and early 1930s, when the Federal Trade
Commission charged that electric utilities pursued monopo-
listic practices and excessive use of public relations. Since
then, the industry has developed a few nervous tics—a
defensive pride in its product, a gnawing fear of more
government regulation, a continued emphasis on public

relations. Nonetheless individual utilities are usually financial and social pillars of their communities—responsible,
interested and often eager to help with planning studies
or grants to cultural institutions. Why then is this great
industry in such deep environmental trouble? The best answer
is that the environmental movement hit the industry on its
blind side, and caught it totally unprepared.

Traditionally, the utilities put their greatest effort into
delivering great blocks of juice at the lowest possible cost.
One accepted way to lower the cost of electricity not so long
ago was to burn cheap coal, which unfortunately happened
also to be "dirty" coal. The customers did not mind the
sulfur and the soot just as long as the price per kilowatt
was kept low. While the utilities polluted their surroundings,
the people flipped their switches, plugged in and twirled their
dials. Everybody was happy. Then the environmental movement came along and changed the ground rules. It demanded
that expensive, low-sulfur coal be burned and that costly
pollution abatement devices be installed — both measures
that would not return one cent on investment. In response,
most utility executives simply shrugged, refusing to heed the
urgent requests for reform.

Why? Perhaps the industry did not think that the movement would last. Some critics suggest an unkinder reason:
they believe that the industry routinely ignores change because it has a monopoly on a coveted product. Besides,
the electric utilities are famous for hiring engineers from the
bottom half of graduating classes; presumably, these men
work up their corporate ladders and eventually occupy top
positions. Even worse, the critics continue, the electric
utilities do not tend to attract bright, innovative outsiders for
two reasons. One is that the industry is heavily regulated by
government, which intrudes into almost every aspect of
business activity, from setting rates to licensing new plants.
The other is that the utilities depend on huge bond issues
to raise most of the money they need for new facilities, and
lenders usually put additional restrictions on the way bor-
rowers conduct their business. As a result, say the critics,

only a special kind of businessman—a solid but unimaginative one — would accept such massive constraints on his autonomy. It stands to reason that this kind of manager would also be reluctant to change his previously successful ways for any social cause, including the environment.

Another, more likely explanation is that environmentalism threatens the fundamental philosophy of the electric utilities more than that of other industries, therefore has to be resisted. The only answer to the dilemmas of power is to reduce per capita consumption of electricity, but growth has always been the watchword of the utilities. Indeed, the industry's established way of business is predicated on growth. Consider the philosophy implied in rate schedules that favor big consumers: the more juice the big consumer uses, the lower the per unit price of electricity. This in turn leads to more demand and another cut in unit prices. Or take another built-in spiral that one insider has described as the two "problems" of the industry: "The first of these is to build demand for our service. The second is to build capacity to meet that demand." Predicting demand years in advance, however, is difficult. If the forecast is too high, the utility will wind up paying heavy fixed costs on a plant whose power is not needed so early. If it is too low, the utility will have to operate old, inefficient plants beyond retirement dates. To help solve the problems, the industry has indulged in aggressive promotional advertising, based of course on the wonders of its product. Consolidated Edison of New York's "Save a Watt" ad campaign, which actually urges conservation of energy, came in 1971 as a momentous break in a hallowed tradition, an admission that growth in demand can be curbed. (Con Ed's lead has since been followed by several other companies.)

Other traditions are now toppling, too. According to the Edison Electric Institute, total revenues from sales to customers in 1969 amounted to $16.5 billion. But only .025 percent of that amount was allotted to research and development—one-tenth the average percentage of gross income spent for such purposes by other U.S. industries. Most of the R & D money went into transmission lines research, which is certainly needed, but not as badly as development of cleaner, more pollution-free generating systems. Some of the industry's leaders see the mistake. Con Ed's chairman, Charles F. Luce, now calls for R & D expenditures "on the order of $200 to $300 million per year," and Lelan Sillin, chairman of Northeast Utilities, has upped the ante to $40 billion during the next thirty years—all for developing clean power.

While such signs of change are heartening, the evidence, alas, is that most utilities have not changed at all. They still denigrate environmentalists as professional rabble-rousers, special interest groups, addled bird watchers, even hinting darkly on occasion that antinuclear critics are agents of the coal industry. When pressed to install antipollution equipment, they still cite the possibility of blackouts (babies dead in hospital incubators, ye gods, mighty factories bereft of motion — frozen, dark and useless). The utilities still believe they have all the facts, therefore the absolute truth. Such stubbornness, carried to extremes, ends up as blindness, as manifest in this *verbatim* excerpt of a letter written in February, 1971, by the advertising manager of Portland General Electric Company to a man wondering about the company's Trojan reactor:

> . . . I really wish I knew what the reasons are for groups like the Citizens for Safe Power or Friends of the Earth to come out with the overstretched, half truth statements as they do and posing as factual. Sometimes—and this is my personal opinion—[I think] that they belong to a different political philosophy than Americans do and are doing things like preventing needed electrical energy to destroy our country. If I were on the other side, I'd follow their footprints of destruction exactly. First I'd get all our kids to use drugs and dress like tramps . . . then I'd start a campaign to convince the populace that nuclear power is a killer. With youth and dwindling energy resources, we'd be ripe for destruction . . .

Equally uncompromising attitudes led to, or appear during, practically every controversy mentioned in this book. The consequent waste of time, effort and money is staggering. Nothern States Power, now one of the most environmentally aware electric utilities, may well have set off a dispute that cost the company millions when, on the theory that a public utility's work is private, it arrogantly dismissed bumbling questions at a public hearing. Or think of what New York State Electric & Gas Company might have avoided (not to mention at least $2 million in lost excavation costs) if it had responded to critics of its proposed nuke with any statement other than that "the Company is not in the business of answering questions from the public."

One of NYSE&G's critics, biologist Alfred W. Eipper, has compiled a list of questions that environmentalists should ask electric utilities:

(1)   Who took part in formulating the assumptions and conclusions about this program's desirability?

(2)   What lasting human benefits will the program provide?

(3)   Who is going to derive such benefits?

(4)   What problems will or may be created?

(5)   What other alternatives exist? In particular, what is the relative desirability of the first alternative: not enacting the program?

In an article in *Science* magazine, Eipper also notes a series of typical industry replies that he describes as "questionable":

(1)   The program—as proposed—*has* to be enacted *now*.

(2)   The program will be enacted in any case. You can't stop progress.

(3)   The program is needed to fill the demand that will be created by the program.

(4)   No one opposed the program. It will benefit the majority and harm no one.

(5)   Data used to estimate effects of the program are the only valid, pertinent data available.

(6)   Since there is no proof that the development will

damage the environment, we can safely assume that it will not.

(7) All effects of the program have been considered.

(8) The program, as presented, represents the sum total of the development contemplated for this particular resource.

(9) All applicable alternatives have been considered.

Confronted with the industry's general refusal to see their point of view, environmentalists have adopted a slogan: "Utilities react to pressure, not logic." The results have been on the whole gratifying.

A typical case involves Commonwealth Edison Company of Chicago. Located on a high floor in Chicago's First National Bank Building, the board room of Commonwealth Edison fits every preconception of what a major utility's inner sanctum should be. Three walls are covered with backlit, colored maps showing service areas and transmission routes, or graphs defining costs and customer configurations. It looks like power, in every sense of the word. Yet the company's annual report of 1970 — the most flattering mirror of its yearly feats — starts with an admission of frailty.

Dear Stockholder:

1970 was the year of the tree, the grass, the air and the water. It was the most difficult so far in my business experience . . .

The words, of course, reflect the rise of citizen concern for the Illinois environment — and the beleaguered company's agonized response.

The company serves eight million customers in an area covering 14,000 square miles. It now has fifteen generating stations (with six more under construction or planned), sending 9,900 megawatts of electricity surging on high voltage interconnections throughout the Midwest. Serious trouble began in 1970 when Commonwealth was officially branded by Chicago's Department of Environmental Control as the city's Number One air polluter. Its stacks spewed 212,574 tons of sulfur dioxide and huge amounts of soot over the city each year. At the company's annual meeting in April, 1970, stockholders urged Commonwealth Edison to review and perhaps revise its environmental policies. Outside the locked meeting room, protesters led by the Rev. Leonard Dubi, a Catholic priest whose church lies in the shadow of the company's Ridgeland plant in southwest Chicago, chanted: "Breathe, let us breathe."

As the protesters knew only too well, Commonwealth burned 20 million tons of coal a year. Most of it came from huge mines in mid-Illinois, and Illinois coal (except some that is completely reserved for metallurgical industries on long-term contracts) is sulfurous. Indeed, its sulfur content of 3.5 percent was too high to meet new Chicago laws designed to curb air pollution. Implemented in July, 1970, the laws set the maximum permissable sulfur content at 1.8 percent with gradual reductions to 1 percent by 1972. At one blow, Commonwealth Edison's traditional supply of fuel was made illegal.

Unable to procure scarce natural gas, the cleanest alternative fuel, Commonwealth tried to buck import restrictions on low-sulfur oil from far away Libya and South America. This move, however, angered influential coal interests in Washington, who feared they might lose lucrative midwestern utility markets if Commonwealth were permitted to set a precedent. In the end, the company was allowed to convert its Ridgeland plant to oil at a cost of $8 million. For the rest of its fuel, though, Commonwealth Edison had to go west, contracting to buy low-sulfur coal from producers in the Rocky Mountains — at double the cost of Illinois coal (including transportation in the company's specially purchased 575 coal hopper railroad cars).

Still, the troubles had just begun. The company found that the western coal did not burn well in its old furnaces, turning instead into what George Travers, Commonwealth's director of environmental studies, calls "something like concrete; we had to chip it out with jackhammers." Moreover, the coal proved to be surprisingly inefficient — that is, it created less B.T.U.'s and more fly ash per ton than Illinois coal. The company therefore had to upgrade the electrostatic precipitators in its smokestacks. These devices, says Travers, now can "remove 98 percent or more of the soot".

Travers hopes Commonwealth Edison can solve its air pollution problems in such a way that it can once again use the cheap, abundant and nearby Illinois coal. The company has three experiments under way. At the Will County station, Commonwealth is spending $7 million to develop a limestone injection system to capture excess sulfur in the smokestacks. "We are pretty sure that it will work," says Travers. "It seems to be 80 percent or better effective on SO_2 and 98 percent effective on fly ash." In another plant, another patented sulfur removal process is now being tested at a cost of $4 million. Even more important, Commonwealth has joined a consortium of gas and electric companies to find a feasible way of turning coal into gas. If successful—a big if, Travers admits—the process will also create "char" which can be burned in power plants and sulfur which might be sold in the marketplace.

"You can't guarantee the results of these experiments," says Travers, "but once we explain them to environmentalists, protests die down. Everybody has been understanding now that we seem to have gotten over the adrenalin phase of environmentalism. Now we're in the gray matter phase. With time, money and brain power, most of the pollution problems can be licked."

Just as Commonwealth Edison's anti-air-pollution drive was spurred mainly by Chicago's new environmental laws, its attack on the problems of nuclear plants has depended every step of the way on the goads of environmentalists. Of the company's four nukes a-building, all have been outfitted in response to citizens' demands with special equipment— recombiners, filters, holding tanks — to keep radioactive releases as close to zero as possible. Travers extols the pressurized reactor being installed at Zion, Illinois, on Lake Michigan. "This is a different kind of animal from boiling water reactors," he says, "because any radiological release goes into the water, not the air. According to the manufacturer, the water will be held captive and recycled — not

released into Lake Michigan. Westinghouse describes it as an
'essentially zero release station.' "

Thermal pollution may be more of a problem for Commonwealth Edison, because like most power companies, it insists
that the hot water that pours from nukes is not necessarily
harmful. In one case, the Illinois Pollution Control Board dis-
agreed and delayed approval of the company's Dresden reactors at the juncture of the Kankakee and Des Plaines rivers
until facilities were built to cool the discharges. But to the
dismay of conservationists, both the Quad Cities reactors on
the Mississippi River and the Zion plant on Lake Michigan
have so far not had to install cooling devices. Local conservationists and Chicago's Metropolitan Sanitary District have
sued Commonwealth Edison, asking that it be made to add
cooling towers at Zion and claiming that the 2,200 megawatt
reactor, one of the biggest on Lake Michigan, probably needs
them more than any other.

Though Commonwealth Edison clearly has made a start on
coping with its environmental problems, it just as clearly has
much left to do. The magnitude of the job ahead was defined in
mid-1972 in a remarkable, year-long study by the Council on
Economic Priorities, a non-profit research organization. Entitled *The Price of Power,* the report assessed the performance
of fifteen electric utilities in installing equipment to control
pollution. Commonwealth Edison was recognized to have especially difficult problems because most of its plants burn coal,
the dirtiest fuel. Even so, reported the Council, "63 percent of
Comm Ed's fossil fuel capacity is inadequately controlled for
particulates, and 76 percent for SO_2." The Council went on to
estimate the cost of putting the most effective available antipollution devices into those plants: about $285.2 million. To
pay that enormous bill, the electric utility would of course have
to pass the costs along to the consumer in rate increases—making the price of electricity reflect environmental as well as economic realities. As Joanna Underwood, the editor of the report, says: "Electric utilities owe the public more than cheap
power. They must now fully accept the responsibility for providing the safest and most reliable power possible and for doing this with the least possible pollution of our air and water
and with the least destruction of our land."

3. Going to Court

Case studies:
Storm King and Calvert Cliffs.

One of the main reasons power plants have earned such public disdain as polluters is surely industry's past, blithe attitude toward the Great Garbage Dump of the environment. Equally important has been the failure of governmental procedures. A regulating agency stands at every step in a power plant's long progress from drawing board to full-blast operation. To get a fossil-fired plant built in New York City, for example, requires the separate approval of three federal, three state, and about twenty city agencies. The trouble is that each agency looks only at that aspect of the plant for which it has direct responsibility — water quality, boiler operation, public health, blasting permit, and so forth. As a result, each has as fragmented a view of the plant as the seven blind men had of the elephant. To make matters worse, the electric utilities have learned to weave their way through — and get their way with — this jumble of juris- dictions. All of which poses a fundamental problem: Who protects the environment?

The courts can help. In his book, *Defending the Environ- ment*, Joseph L. Sax, himself a lawyer, describes one major way: "In the ever expanding and elaborate procedures that the legislatures impose on administrative agencies, it is usually rather easy to find some procedural blunder or failing that can be called to the attention of a court." The vulnerable procedures include such things as holding hearings, making studies or reports, and consulting with other agencies. If a procedure has not been followed, the court merely sends the case back to the agency, telling it to reform.

A famous case in this regard is technically known as Scenic Hudson Preservation Conference *v.* Federal Power Commission or, to most people simply as *Storm King*. It began in 1963 when Consolidated Edison Company of New York applied to the Federal Power Commission, which oversees all hydroelectric projects, for a license to build a two-million-kilowatt hydroplant on the Hudson River near Cornwell, fifty miles upstream from New York City.

The plant would not be just an ordinary one but a special kind called "pumped storage." To be located at the base of 1,400-foot Storm King Mountain, the facility would suck six billion gallons of water through a two-mile-long tunnel up to a 240-acre man-made reservoir in a nearby high valley. When Con Ed needed power to meet peak demands in New York City, it would simply pull the plug, so to speak, and the falling water would spin the turbines before flowing back into the Hudson. Then at night, when demand for electricity dropped to its lowest level, the company would use the power from other generating stations to supply energy for the Storm King plant to pump water back up to the reservoir. Though this pumping process would use three kilowatts of power for every two the plant would later be able to generate, those three off-hour kilowatts were cheap while the two peak-hour kilowatts could be sold dearly.

All this sounds ingenious, sensible, and neat, especially since hydro plants create no air or conventional water pollution. But there is a rub. Almost by definition, any locale consisting of heights overlooking a major body of water is scenic, and Storm King is beyond scenic. So overwhelming is the granite mountain on the river narrows that conservationists united into the Scenic Hudson Preservation Conference to keep it unspoiled. Led masterfully by publicist Rod Vandivert, they defended the mountain while attacking Con Ed with broadside after broadside of angry letters, press releases and public warnings about unsightly transmission lines. Con Ed's own public relations team replied by calling its critics "misinformed bird watchers, nature fakers, land grabbers, and militant adversaries of progress." On hearing that, a well-born conservationist named Pierre Ledoux decisively capped it with a reference to the company: "Yes, I am a bird watcher," he said, "and I have been watching buzzards and vultures."

The details of the Storm King controversy have been recounted so often and vividly as to be unnecessary here. (Among the best descriptions are chapters in two good books, Gene Marine's *America the Raped* and Robert H. Boyle's *The Hudson River*.) In outline, though, the Federal Power Commission in 1965 granted Con Edison a permit to build the plant, and the conservationists immediately sought redress in court—helping to establish, in the process, all environmentalists' "standing" in court (the ability to sue even though the plaintiffs or their property are not directly involved in the outcome). They argued that the plant would ruin scenic values at the mountain and around the reservoir as well as kill billions of fish eggs and larvae sucked from the Hudson. Thus, their lawyers (most notably David Sive) charged that the Federal Power Commission had neither adequately considered the adverse effects of the plant, nor had explored alternative methods of generating the needed power (mainly gas-fired turbines).

On December 29, 1965, the U.S. Court of Appeals handed down a caustically worded opinion:

In this case, as in many others, the Commission has claimed to be the representative of the public interest. This role does not permit it to act as an umpire blandly calling balls and strikes for adversaries appearing before it; the right of the public must receive active and affirmative protection at the hands of the

Commission . . . The Commission must see to it that
the record is complete . . . Renewed proceedings must
include as a basic concern the preservation of natural
beauty and of national historic shrines, keeping in mind
that, in our affluent society, the cost of a project is only
one of several factors to be considered.

When Bob Boyle heard that the court had sent the proposal back to the FPC for further hearing, he wrote, "I
was only one of many people who got riotously drunk."

But the case was not resolved by a long shot. In attempts
to preserve the scenery, Con Ed pledged to bury its plant
underground, build lookouts and a riverside park. It also
promised to protect fish, though no fishermen could believe
that would be possible. Even so, the conservationists' main
point still remained. Any project would desecrate the
mountain. Of Storm King's grandeur, a Yale art historian
named Vincent Scully said:

It rises like a brown bear out of the river, a dome of
living granite, swelling with animal power. It is not
picturesque in the softer sense of the word but awesome,
a primitive embodiment of the energies of the earth . . .
the urbanistic point of the Hudson in that area lies in
the fact that it preserves and embodies the most savage
and wild at the very threshold of New York. It can
still make the city dweller emotionally aware of what he
needs to know: that nature still exists, with its own laws,
rhythms, and powers, separate from human desires.

Nonetheless, the FPC's hearing examiner in 1968 again
recommended that the pumped storage plant be licensed,
and in August, 1970, the FPC approved the project again.
Further litigation by the Scenic Hudson group (now 20,000
members strong) will delay the project further—or kill it
forever.

Since the storm broke over Storm King, a few states have
empowered a high-level agency, usually a Public Service
Commission (which regulates rates) to try to supply a needed
environmental perspective on new electric generating projects.
Unfortunately, such efforts are not only few in number but

all too often weak in effect. But in 1969 Congress passed the Big Bertha of environmental law, the National Environmental Policy Act, signed by President Nixon on January 1, 1970. With NEPA, as the act is known, the federal government pledged to consider the environment before plunging ahead with any project. Specifically, the act requires all federal agencies to describe in detail all facets of a project's environmental impact, including avoidable adverse effects and possible alternative courses of action.

NEPA dealt environmentalists a new hand of cards. It provided a means of at least challenging new generating stations by questioning impact statements, for many federal agencies besides the Federal Power Commission deal with energy. The U.S. Army Corps of Engineers often dredges channels or builds dikes for power plants. Most important, though, is the Atomic Energy Commission, which oversees licensing, construction and operations of nuclear plants.

Of the federal bureaucracies, the AEC is perhaps the most frequently attacked. The electric utilities charge that it is overly conservative and moves with the exaggerated caution of an old lady on an icy street. When Portland General Electric applied for permission to build a nuke on the shores of the Columbia River, for example, the AEC made the utility plan against the possibility of an eruption of a virtually extinct volcano fifty miles away. On the other hand, environmentalists criticize the agency on a number of grounds, starting with the fact that it both promotes and regulates nuclear programs—clearly a conflict of interest. What bothers them even more is the AEC's refusal ever to consider any effects of nuclear power plants on the environment except those involving radiation. Moreover, the AEC has ignored the protests of citizens groups that want to participate in licensing hearings by excluding them entirely, or questioning the extent and effectiveness of their participation.

Though NEPA seemed to apply equally to all federal agencies, the AEC almost arbitrarily decided it need not obey that law until March, 1971. To test that decision— and the AEC's environmental responsibilities—three conservation groups haled the agency to court in mid-1970. The case concerned a huge, controversial nuclear plant a-building in Maryland at Calvert Cliffs, sixty miles south of Baltimore on Chesapeake Bay. It turned out to be a Son of Storm King.

The Calvert Cliffs story really began back in 1967, when Baltimore Gas & Electric Company (BG & E) announced it was "going nuclear" with a new 1,600-megawatt plant, a decision determined solely by economics. Though the enormous facility would cost 10 percent more than a comparable coal-fueled plant, its operating expenses would be lower. Besides, BG & E's chairman said, "We won't have any bulky fuel storage areas. The plant will be attractive and clean." That statement tells a lot about the purely cosmetic attention the environment got in those days.

As usual, the residents around Calvert Cliffs did not have anything to say in the decision to have a tremendous nuke as neighbor. Outraged, they sought strength in numbers and organized into the Chesapeake Environmental Protection Association in early 1969. Their first challenge was the planned route of high-tension wires to the nuclear facility. While the citizens emphatically opposed tall utility towers stalking through their landscape, they also had to face practical facts. And the facts were that the company owned the plant site plus some of the line's right-of-way. And with power shortages looming in the future the electricity had to go to the market, did it not? Even so, the citizens had to wonder how the company could be so confident the plant would be built. A little research revealed that BG & E had no construction permit from the AEC, no "certificate of public convenience and necessity" from the Maryland Public Service Commission, no permit from the state to allow use of Chesapeake Bay water for cooling. It seemed a bit odd—not to say arrogant—that BG & E was nonetheless digging into its site as if all the permits were as good as granted.

At the AEC's public hearings for a construction permit in 1969, the citizens tried to rouse the bureaucratic conscience. But when they questioned the possibly harmful effects of pumping heated water into a part of the bay that one citizen called "the greatest fishing hole in the nation," the AEC just listened sympathetically and repeated the familiar line that thermal pollution was not within its jurisdiction. Instead the problem should be brought up before Maryland's Department of Water Resources. Nor would AEC procedures allow presentation of testimony regarding the choice of the plant's location or the relationship between size of the plant and the actual power needs to be served. Under law, the AEC insisted that it could only judge questions involving health, safety and national security pertaining to actual construction of the plant.

Who protected the environment? A group of scientists from John Hopkins University warned that low-level radio-active emissions from the plant might well prove dangerous to human health. The Maryland Academy of Sciences studied the possible environmental effects of the plant and concluded, with curious logic, that the nuke should serve as an "experimental tool" in assessing the eventual impact of more nuclear plants on the environment of the Chesapeake Bay region. Jess W. Malcolm, executive director of the Chesapeake Bay Foundation, Inc., summarized the real problem. He counted thirty separate actions by different agencies. "The decision," he said acidly, "is being made in a series of minor decisions suggesting de facto approval of the facility every step of the way. All of these steps were taken when, in fact, the basic question of whether a plant that would use Chesapeake Bay waters should be constructed was never even asked." Needless to say, the AEC with its limited perspective granted the plant a construction permit.

The next public hearing in 1969 was before the Maryland Public Service Commission to decide if the commission had the right to review the Calvert Cliffs plant's history. A legal nicety was involved. In a fit of enlightenment the Maryland legislature had given the PSC the critical ability to pass on the state's new power plant siting, construction and operating plans. Unfortunately, however, the PSC's authority began two months after BG & E had started preparing the site in

1968. Did those two months allow the plant to escape the PSC's review? The state commission finally decided it, too, lacked jurisdiction in the case. Arguing that site-work was not really "construction," citizens promptly took the question of the PSC's statutory authority before the courts. Meantime, construction of the nuclear plant continued.

By then the National Environmental Policy Act provided the opportunity for the Sierra Club, National Wildlife Federation and Calvert Cliffs Coordinating Council to plead that the AEC was unequivocally responsible for taking a broad environmental view of the nuke. This contention—like Storm King, a question of procedure—also went before the courts. One of the lawyers on the case, Anthony Z. Roisman, recalls the moment. "There is no enemy as easy to attack as an ogre," he says, "and the AEC was getting that reputation. The public clearly wanted to participate in decisions about power plants and the AEC was not letting them."

As Calvert Cliffs boiled into national prominence, Senator Edmund Muskie had his say. At a Senate subcommittee hearing in 1970 on his own power plant siting bill, he leaned forward and challenged a statement by Baltimore Gas & Electric's chairman, C.E. Utermohle. What the utility chief seemed to be saying, Muskie rumbled, was that "momentum already built into the decision-making process is such that, in effect, we are foreclosed from taking additional steps to safeguard the environment . . ." But the state itself proved Muskie's fears mistaken. First the Maryland Department of Water Resources gave the Calvert Cliffs plant a water-use permit sparkling with twenty-one severe restrictions to protect the environment. Later the Public Service Commission, by then awarded authority over the plant by the courts, issued a "certificate of public convenience and necessity" unlike any other elsewhere. PSC chairman William O. Doub commented: "This plant will operate under the most stringent conditions and standards in the country." BG & E had not only to install devices to cut radioactive emissions far below AEC standards. It also had to report on the ecology of Chesapeake

Bay and the Calvert Cliffs plant's impact on the local environment.

In July, 1971, the U.S. Court of Appeals for the District of Columbia ruled on the conservation groups' suit against the AEC. The decision was an environmentalist's dream. It defined NEPA in strong unambiguous terms, saying that the act's language "does not provide an escape hatch for foot-dragging agencies; it does not make NEPA's procedural requirements somehow 'discretionary.' Congress did not intend the act to be such a paper tiger." Indeed, the court continued, "we believe that the Atomic Energy Commission's crabbed interpretation of NEPA makes a mockery of the act."

The court's caustic words recalled the Storm King decision. In ruling that NEPA makes environmental protection a basic part of the AEC's mandate, the court said:

The primary responsibility for fulfilling that mandate lies with the Commission. Its responsibility is not simply to sit back, like an umpire, and resolve adversary contentions at the hearing stage. Rather it must itself take the initiative of considering environmental values at every distinctive and comprehensive stage of the process beyond the staff's evaluation and recommendation.

The court then removed all the procedural roadblocks that the AEC had erected in the way of serious public participation in licensing hearings for new nuclear plants. Nor could the commission exclude environmental factors from the hearings by shifting those responsibilities to other state and federal agencies. In fact, the decision declared that the AEC is not prevented "from demanding water pollution controls from its licensees which are more strict than those demanded by the applicable water quality standards of the certifying agencies." In other words, qualified environmentalists can properly raise questions at AEC hearings (or in court) about thermal pollution, fish kills and even siting. The decision's main impact will thus be on nuclear plants yet to be built.

How about the nukes already under construction? The

opinion, written by Judge J. Skelly Wright with Judges Edward A. Tamm and Spottswood W. Robinson III concurring, dealt with the AEC's argument that it had needed fourteen months of delay before complying with NEPA because nuclear power plants were urgently needed to solve the nation's "energy crisis." The court retorted: "Whether or not the spectre of a national power crisis is as real as the Commission apparently believes, it must not be used to create a blackout of the environmental consideration in the agency review process." Thus, the court declared that the AEC had to make detailed environmental impact statements on all fifty-two nuclear plants started or finished since NEPA took effect—including, of course, the Calvert Cliffs nuke.

This would pose some problems. The court said: "In cases where environmental costs were not considered in granting a construction permit, it is very likely that the planned facility will include some features which do significant damage to the environment and which could not have survived [the] rigorous balancing of costs and benefits" that NEPA demands. Waiting until construction is finished and the utility seeks an operating license, the court added, means that "either the licensee will have to undergo a major expense in making alterations in a completed facility or the environmental harm will have to be tolerated. It is all too probable that the latter result would come to pass." Therefore, the court advised the AEC to "consider very seriously the requirement of a temporary halt in construction pending its review and the 'backfitting' of technological innovations."

In summary, the court has defined the procedures that NEPA imposes on all federal agencies. Now there is ample opportunity for citizens to combat power plants in a way which, while not promoting a final solution, certainly helps to protect the environment. Perhaps the most important aspect of the Calvert Cliffs decision is the suggestion that if a project's adverse environmental effects outweigh its economic benefits, it ought to be stopped. That conclusion, however, remains to be tested in another case, maybe—why not?—somewhere in the continuing litigation over Storm King.

Postscript:

Between the time of writing this chapter and the press deadline, Dr. James R. Schlesinger replaced Dr. Glenn T. Seaborg as chairman of the AEC. One of Schlesinger's first acts was to decide against appealing the Calvert Cliffs decision to a higher court. He thus accepted the AEC's responsibility for considering the environmental impact of all nuclear plants, fifty-two others under construction, and thirty-one on the drawing boards. If the industry was figuratively shocked by that, another surprise was soon to come. Schlesinger spelled out the AEC's role, telling industry representatives: "You should not expect the AEC to fight the industry's political, social and commercial battles. The AEC exists to serve the public interest."

In late October 1971, the Storm King controversy also entered a new phase. A federal court, by a vote of two to one, sustained a Federal Power Commission license for Con Edison to build a proposed pumped-storage plant at Storm King. The Scenic Hudson Preservation Conference pledged to continue its legal battle against the project, both in state and federal courts. One ground: the FPC had not adequately followed the mandates of NEPA as defined in the Calvert Cliffs decision.

4. The Dawning of the Nuclear Age

Case study:
Bodega Head.

On September 6, 1954, ground-breaking ceremonies for the United States' first commercial-sized (sixty-seven-megawatt) nuclear power plant took place in Shippingport, Pennsylvania. President Dwight D. Eisenhower, though not present, commented that he saw, in the development of the peaceful atom, mankind coming "closer to fulfillment on a new and better earth". Most Americans tended to agree. Enthralled by the technological fervor of the times, they took the Shippingport nuke as a wondrous symbol of implacable progress.

On the other hand, the word "nuclear" also evoked a vision of August 6, 1945, and a solitary U.S. warplane called the *Enola Gay* droning over Hiroshima with a cargo of one bomb. Dropped from 32,000 feet, that bomb created a fireball 110 yards in diameter which briefly reached 300,000 degrees centigrade, sufficient to melt surfaces off granite 1,000 yards away. Then the mushroom cloud billowed up 50,000 feet. Many other people remembered the Japanese fishing vessel *Lucky Dragon*. Unlucky enough to be seventy-two miles off a Marshall Island A-bomb testing site in March, 1954, the boat was dusted with white radioactive ash. Soon thereafter, the crew was stricken ill and made for home and hospitalization. When one fisherman died the following September a point about radiation had been made. As Harry Slater, an executive of Niagara Mohawk Power Corporation was to say, the peaceful atom's first problem was that it was "conceived in secrecy, born in warfare, developed in fear."

The problem was not adroitly handled. In 1957, just before the Shippingport reactor went into operation, the AEC released a document entitled "Theoretical Possibilities and Consequences of Major Accidents in Large Nuclear Power Plants." Researched by AEC scientists at the Brookhaven National Laboratory, the report attempted to answer two questions: (1) what is the likelihood of a major reactor accident; and (2) what would be the consequences of such an accident? The scientists took as a hypothetical case a 100- to 200-megawatt reactor in a suburban location near a large body of water about thirty miles from a city of one million people. They then assumed that everything went wrong at the precise moment when the plant had built up the maximum amount of radioactive products. "It is as if someone were to try to figure what would happen if every nut, bolt and other structural support suddenly broke in New York's Pan Am Building and that the building fell into Grand Central Station at rush hour," says Paul Turner of the Atomic Industrial Forum, an industry group. "The situation is obviously impossible." Indeed, scientists pointed out that the possibility of the hypothetical accident was so remote as to be near the vanishing point. One reason: the radioactive products would somehow have to escape a succession of physical barriers within the plant. Another: every additional safety feature—e.g., core spray and containment spray systems—would also have to fail.

Despite such qualifications, the report's conclusions were all too simple: if 50 percent of the hypothetical plant's fission products were released to the atmosphere, 3,400 people would be killed and 43,000 injured within a radius of forty-five miles. In addition, property damage within an area of up to 150,000 square miles would exceed $7 billion.

The figures, if not their context, were chilling—very bad public relations. Nuclear power plants were to grow much larger than 200 megawatts and be sited closer to cities than thirty miles.

The reason the study was made in the first place was to help to determine the limits of insurance for nuclear plants. Yet by itself, the insurance industry was unwilling to enter the area. In 1956, Herbert W. Yount, vice-president of Liberty Mutual Insurance Company, told the Joint Congressional Committee on Atomic Energy:

> The catastrophe hazard is apparently many times as great as anything previously known in the industry . . . We have heard estimates of catastrophe potential under the worst possible circumstances running not merely into millions or tens of millions but into hundreds of millions and billions of dollars. It is a reasonable question of public policy as to whether a hazard of this dimension should be permitted, if it actually exists. Obviously there is no principle of insurance which can be applied to a single location where the potential loss approaches such astronomical proportions. Even if insurance could be found, there is serious question whether the amount of damages to persons and property would be worth the possible benefit accruing from atomic development.

Still, the electric utilities were not going to develop atomic power without adequate insurance. To resolve the dilemma in 1957, the federal government stepped in with an act named after its sponsors, Congressman Melvin Price and Senator Clinton Anderson, both members of the Joint Committee. As originally enacted, the Price-Anderson Act forces every reactor operator to buy all available maximum insurance from private companies ($60 million in 1957, subsequently raised to $82 million), above which ceiling the federal government would supply another $500 million of coverage (subsequently lowered to $478 million).

Inevitably, critics compared the Brookhaven report's theoretical damages of $7 billion with the Price-Anderson

Act's limit of $560 million. It required little imagination to conclude that in its insurance the private utilities were being subsidized by taxpayers and that, no matter how horrendous an accident might be, the utilities would not suffer any financial loss. The fact that the electric utilities have had an excellent record—there have been only sixteen minor incidents involving insurance to date—does not in any way vitiate the critics' argument. The act provides an umbrella for the utilities' operations, inasmuch as they would be unwilling to build nuclear reactors without it.

From 1957 to 1962, small nuclear plants were planned, built and put into operation at such places as Morris, Illinois; Rowe, Massachusetts; and Buchanan, New York. Though each plant was clearly experimental, each community warmly welcomed the nuclear neighbor. The only significant exception was a peculiar project in northern California. Like the rumble of distant thunder, the happenings at Bodega Bay gave warning that the nuclear program was in for trouble.

To millions of Americans, Bodega Bay, California, is familiar as the setting for Alfred Hitchcock's movie, *The Birds*. Hitchcock himself was enchanted by the little fishing village of Bodega and its protected bay—the safest harbor of refuge between San Francisco, 50 miles to the south, and Coos Bay, Oregon, 250 miles north along a rugged, often forbidding coastline. When the film maker first saw the area in the early 1960s he pronounced it "a rare find, remote and unspoiled by man." In a word, it was perfect for his purposes.

Hitchcock was not the first to reach that conclusion. Ever since 1944 California's Division of Beaches and Parks had wanted land around Bodega for the state parks system. In particular, the division wanted Bodega Head, a peninsula which hooks sharply from the mainland of Sonoma County two miles out into the Pacific Ocean. In 1956, the University of California began negotiating with Beaches and Parks to get some land on Bodega Head for a marine laboratory. Indeed, it was an unique site. Two unpolluted ecosystems were set on each side of the peninsula: On the bay, tidal mud flats teemed with cockle, clam, shrimp and myriad other aquatic creatures. On the ocean frontage were tide pools alive with anemones, starfish, abalone, mussels and snails. But in 1957, both the university and Beaches and Parks dropped their plans. Pacific Gas & Electric (PG & E) the nation's second largest power company, had also found Bodega.

What did PG & E see in the area that took precedence over a state park or research facility? Although company officials did not spell out the answer until 1961, Bodega Head seemed to be the perfect place for a nuclear power plant. Close to the company's largest industrial customers around San Francisco, the peninsula was also safely isolated from centers of population. Moreover, the harbor would allow easy shipment of heavy generating equipment by sea. Once built, the $61-million, 325-megawatt plant could gulp great draughts of bay water for cooling and then discharge the heated water into the ocean, where natural turbulence would quickly disperse the heat. Inland, dairy ranches covered the rolling hills—just the kind of open countryside that is ideal for transmission lines. Even geology seemed to be on PG & E's side. A company engineer testified at a public hearing: "The natural granite rock foundation for the plant provides an ideally stable platform." He was to be proven wrong.

Between 1957 and 1962 PG & E quietly developed its plans. Few citizens protested. One who spoke out was oceanographer Joel Hedgpeth; he liked nothing about PG & E's plans and said so in public, disregarding vague threats to his career at the University of the Pacific. Another was Rose Gaffney, a major landowner on Bodega Head who did not want to lose her property to a power company. "I am not asking for your sympathy," she later said speaking for all landowners threatened with eminent domain. "I am asking for justice."

But in general, people were quiet. Perhaps they were entranced by the prospect of the high taxes that PG & E would pay in the area. More likely, they were silent because they had precious little opportunity to object in a meaningful way. PG & E seldom gave any advance warning of its plans. Worse, the Sonoma County Board of Supervisors, which had to pass on all land-use proposals connected with the project, routinely made public decisions in private and then simply announced the results. For example, the residents of Bodega Bay suddenly learned that their airstrip was to be removed from nearby Doran Park because planes might be endangered by tall transmission towers and lines that were not yet approved or built. So complete was the early exclusion of citizen participation that it took U.S. Congressman Clem Miller's active intercession in 1962 to get the first public hearings in the area—and those hearings did not concern the power plant but an access road to it.

Still, when citizens did have the chance to attend three days of public hearings in March, 1962, before California's Public Utilities Commission, hardly any objectors turned out. But then the PUC started receiving letters of protest urging that the lovely peninsula not be taken for a nuclear plant. In response, the PUC announced it would reopen hearings.

All at once, the opposition found both its voice and the vital asset of an indefatigable leader. David Pesonen, a forester by training, established a 2,000-member citizens group with the awesome name of the Northern California Association to Preserve Bodega Head and Harbor, Inc. For the next two years, it fought the nuclear plant through each step of the licensing process. When that failed, Pesonen's group turned to the courts and to the press. While he succeeded in starting a steady drumbeat of opposition, PG & E pressed ahead with the project. It dug what became known as "the hole in the Head," a pit 140 feet in diameter and 70 feet deep which was designed to hold the nuclear reactor. Excavated rock went into construction of an access road across the bay's tidal flats. The road destroyed much of the mud flats' wildlife values.

In retrospect, it is easy to separate the basic arguments

against the power plant into distinct categories, each of them an important harbinger of controversies yet to come. At first, aesthetics were the main issue: should Bodega Head ever be developed? "The proposed reactor will take a priceless scenic resource for its site, but will produce nothing but common kilowatts," the Sierra Club argued in a "friend of the court" brief. Dave Pesonen tellingly compared the PG & E project to using Yosemite Falls for a hydroelectric project. In 1963, California's Lieutenant Governor Glenn Anderson said that the company's "massive facility" would "permanently scar one of the nation's truly unique, and particularly appealing coastal regions."

But if such an argument rests squarely on the side of the angels—who can object to beauty?—it also depends on the eye of the beholder. PG & E gleefully collected newspapermen's on-the-spot descriptions of Bodega and its surroundings: "a seaside slum," "ugly," "desolate," "inaccessible." The company also noted that California ranked Bodega ninety-third of 123 possible park sites—a low priority which presumably spoke volumes about the area's real esthetic appeal, but may equally have reflected practical factors.

A related and somewhat less subjective debate took the Bodega reactor as a symptom of California's slapdash preparations for the future. Conservation writer Karl Kortum testified: "There is only one population curve that bears on the situation wholly—and that is 17 million people in our state in 1963 and 45 million in our state 37 years later. Forty-five million desperate people—not desperate for more kilowatts but desperate for space, for nature, for the sea, for room for the soul."

Dr. Daniel Luten, a geographer at the University of California, also looked ahead as he dealt specifically with the power company's enticements of new tax revenues, new growth, new progress for Bodega:

You are being told that this power plant will increase the tax base, and it will, of course. And you are either told or left to infer that it will therefore lower your taxes. There was a time when all of us were inclined to believe that if we could increase our tax base, God would provide that no increase in costs would accompany it. Now we know better. All of the rapidly growing parts of the country have increased in tax bases. Are these the areas with the lowest taxes? No, they aren't.

Luten then pinpointed the real problem, one that was to serve as a basis for a whole series of new environmental laws:

Let me ask you the general question, "Does this society exist merely to serve its economy?" No one will answer yes to this question, yet by and large our decisions on public policy are made primarily or wholly in terms of economic considerations. This is attractive because it submits to quantitative analysis. There is a strong and recurring tendency, when both economic and social considerations are involved, to dismiss the social considerations because they cannot be expressed quantitatively and cannot be measured up side by side with the economic terms. But if a society does not exist to serve its economy, such procedure is improper and intolerable.

What lent such arguments special cogency was the fact that the public agencies with some authority over the project neglected to consider anything except limited issues. The Sonoma Board of Supervisors, the state Public Utilities, the AEC—each considered a few of the problems involved and dismissed the others with a shrug as if to say, "Sorry, it's not within our jurisdiction." In this process, the environment was completely neglected. Nor was the utility about to provide the missing perspective. At a remarkable public meeting in 1962, physicist Richard Sill pointed out: "The Pacific Gas & Electric Company, one must remember, is not a philanthropy, and while service is their business, profit is correctly their motive."

Then how could ordinary citizens gain technical competence to contest the reactor proposal? Dr. Sill knew the answer: *"You cannot find out for yourself."*

When the project's opponents searched for information on

the risks of having a reactor in their backyard, what they discovered frightened them. Oceanographer Joel Hedgpeth conceded no one could predict with certainty the effects of the plant's discharge of at least 250,000 gallons of hot water per minute into the Pacific Ocean. Under certain conditions, like a period of calm water and no circulation, he warned, "A tiny thing like this could kill off organic life along several miles of seacoast." More significant, the reactor—biggest to date—was "experimental." Looking over the history of nuclear plants did not reassure them that the Bodega reactor would be safe. They quickly discovered that there had been 300 reactor accidents in the world. Though most were minor, an incident in 1961 at the Arco reactor in Idaho had killed three operating personnel. In another accident at Canada's Chalk River installation, 900 safety devices did not prevent a concurrence of mechanical defects and operating errors resulting in severe damage to the reactor.

Adding to the understandable fears was a certain amount of equally understandable anger. The critics noted that PG & E's announcement to build a nuclear plant closely followed the Atomic Energy Commission's decision to cut the costs of enriched uranium fuel by 34 percent—in effect, a subsidy of nuclear power. Similarly, the Price-Anderson Act of 1957 seemed an unfair indemnification of the hazards of nuclear reactors because the burden of potential losses would be borne by the taxpayer. "We have been launched headlong into the peaceful atom program," David Pesonen argued a little helplessly, "not by reason but by insurance policy."

Fortunately for opponents of the Bodega reactor, there was one issue that was wide open to specific debate. The plant would be built near the San Andreas Fault, the most active earthquake area in the United States. Just how near was important. PG & E engineers reckoned that it would be 1¼ miles from the fault itself and 1,000 feet from the western edge of the fault zone. They insisted that the reactor would be designed to withstand any earthquake, even one as severe as the 1906 tremor that ruined parts of San Francisco and caused Bodega Head itself, an old-time resident remembered, to "roll like the ocean." Moreover, PG & E geologists maintained that the land had withstood countless numbers of earthquakes with virtually no movement.

All this scarcely assuaged public fears. Troubled by the thought of routine radioactive emissions into the air over the dairy farms, numerous mothers picketed PG & E headquarters in what became known as "the Mudders and Udders for pure milk." The specter of a quake causing a much more massive, if accidental, release of radioactivity loomed large. With the help of some friends, one opponent of the plant, jazz trumpeter Lu Watters, released about a thousand helium-filled balloons from Bodega Head on Memorial Day 1963. To each was attached a tag reading "This balloon could represent a radioactive molecule of strontium 90 or iodine 131—tell your local newspaper where you found this balloon." Some drifted as far as populous San Rafael and Richmond.

PG & E quickly denounced the event as "not a scientific experiment, but a publicity stunt." But the company soon got some bad scientific news. The Scripps Institution of Oceanography found a new complex of bedrock faults ninety feet seaward of Bodega Head. Another geologist reported that what the company had thought to be a thick pad of granite under the reactor was really sixty feet of silt, clay and sand.

In October, 1964, the Atomic Energy Commission's Division of Reactor Licensing released its official report:

In our view, the proposal to rely on unproven and perhaps unprovable design measures to cope with forces as great as would be several feet of ground movement under a larger reactor building in a severe earthquake raises substantial safety questions . . . It is our conclusion that Bodega Head is not a suitable location for the proposed nuclear power plant at the present state of our knowledge.

"We have repeatedly stated," responded PG & E President Robert H. Gerdes, "that if any reasonable doubt exists about the safety of the proposed Bodega plant, we would

not consider going forward with it." He therefore canceled
the project, reaping abundant praise for acting in the public
interest. The company had spent between $3 to $4 million
at Bodega Head.

The electric utility industry chose to dismiss the whole
Bodega incident because it was so "specialized." The AEC,
industry leaders were to rationalize, would never, ever, have
licensed such a poorly sited plant. But if that were true, why
did the AEC allow the situation to snowball for so many
months? Whatever the answer may be, the industry was
much more interested in other, minor facets of the case.
Nuclear News magazine implied that a relatively small
number of people—most of them "nonlocal"—clearly did
not have the real facts, i.e., did not believe PG & E's assurances of safety. What really interested the magazine was not
the merits of the critics' case but where they got their funds.
"It is impossible to impute motives to others," the magazine
saw fit to comment, "but those close to the situation feel
that most of the deep-rooted opposition was from ultraliberal
groups who fervently champion federally owned power as
opposed to privately financed power."

The nuclear industry bloomed as if nothing had happened
at Bodega. Economics was the main reason. Nukes seemed
cheaper to operate and fuel than conventional fossil-fired
plants. In a euphoria, power companies ordered so many new
reactors between 1964 and 1966 that *Electric World*
magazine predicted that 56 percent of all generating equipment to come on line between 1971 and 1975 would be
nuclear. The coal companies, beginning to worry about the
future of their best market, put pressure on railroads to
reduce rates for hauling coal to the electric utilities. Even
the supercautious AEC was moved to make a prediction.
By 1970, it said, there would be 11,500 megawatts of
installed nuclear generating capacity. Of course, that forecast
depended on everything going well, from the national economy to public acceptance of nukes.

Yet problems have plagued the industry. Equipment manufacturers fell behind schedule in making deliveries. Construc-

tion of nuclear plants took longer than expected. Inflation sent all costs spiraling. Sales of new reactors slowed. And environmentalists started to revive the doubts raised first at Bodega Bay.

5. Isotopes and Hogwash

Case study:
Monticello.

Though a certain amount of background radiation has always existed in nature, the basic fact is that radiation is extremely dangerous. In large quantities it kills swiftly; in smaller doses it causes cancer in present populations and genetic defects in future ones. The Federal Radiation Council has reported: "There are insignificant data to provide a firm basis for evaluating radiation effects for all types and levels of radiation. There is particular uncertainty with respect to the biological effects of very low doses and dose rates. It is not prudent therefore to assume that there is absolute certainty that no effect may occur." The council laid the cornerstone for establishing U.S. radiation standards in this statement: "There should not be any man-made radiation without the expectation of benefit resulting from such exposure."

Many environmentalists have argued cogently that since such a concept of risk and benefit ends up involving subjective choice rather than scientific certainty, the affected public should be allowed at least to participate in the decision to allow a nuclear plant into its community. The AEC, however, sets national standards for maximum permissible doses of radioactivity. These limits are based on the Federal Radiation Council's national guidelines, which in turn consider the recommendations of both the National Council on Radiation Protection and Measurements, and the International Commission on Radiation Protection. As the nuclear age entered the late 1960s, the limit for exposure to ionizing radiation was established at 170 millirems per year (a millirem is 1/1,000 of a rem) over and above natural background radiation—roughly the equivalent of four chest x-rays a year. It is worth remembering that all nuclear plants operating at the time threw off less radiation than this maximum.

Was that an adequate safeguard? The industry insisted it was. Pressed for more specific information, industry spokesmen responded with such vague comparisons as "the average American is annually exposed to more radiation from sitting in front of his TV set than from a nuclear plant." Most antinuke critics have refused to be convinced by bland assurances. After all, if there was no "safe" level of exposure to radiation, then even 170 millirems was sure to do damage. In 1969, two scientists at the AEC's Lawrence Livermore Laboratory quantified this fear. Dr.'s John W. Gofman and Arthur R. Tamplin announced that if all Americans were annually exposed to 170 millirems of radiation, there would be an increase of 32,000 deaths from cancer each year. They therefore asked that the AEC reduce the limits by a factor of ten.

The calculations and the logic were soon disputed by other scientists—how could *all* Americans be so exposed? —but Gofman and Tamplin took their thesis before a public avid for intelligible, objective information. Their conclusions, while possibly incorrect, and their continuous criticism of the AEC were important factors in moving the United States toward a needed reduction in radiation standards. Even more significant was the Monticello case.

It is ironic that one of the most important nuclear controversies grew directly out of a power company's enforced awareness of environmental problems. During 1964, Northern States Power (NSP), Minnesota's biggest electric utility, had been roasted both locally and in the national press for its most recent big coal-fired facility on the St. Croix River. Part of the problem was that private boat owners also liked the stretch of river that they would have to share with the plant; another part had to do with thermal pollution; and finally there was a fiercer than usual debate over transmission lines. The whole incident was extremely embarrassing to the company and NSP wanted to avoid a repetition.

When the company found in 1965 that it needed additional generating capacity, it decided to go nuclear. Nukes were then being touted as environmentally "clean" because they do not cause the familiar sorts of air pollution. Better yet, they seemed especially economic. The two major equipment manufacturers, Westinghouse and General Electric, were contracting to build not only the reactor itself but the entire plant at favorable—and fixed—costs. After carefully picking a remote, nonrecreational site at Monticello, thirty-four miles up the Mississippi River from Minneapolis and St. Paul, NSP in 1966 signed an $82-million contract with GE for a 545-megawatt boiling water reactor. With the scribble of executive signatures, the company effectively slipped from the fossil frying pan into the nuclear fire.

"It is difficult to determine now exactly when it was that organized opposition developed to the plant," an NSP official named Bjorn Bjornson was later to recall. "Maybe it stemmed from the precocious plumber who first spoke out against the plant at an early AEC hearing. Or it may have started with the bearded professor who took pot shots at us from his ivory tower."

Dr. Dean E. Abrahamson, luxuriously bearded and an associate professor of anatomy and laboratory medicine at the University of Minnesota, might never have gotten even vaguely interested in the Monticello plant had it not been for some questions first raised by the Minnesota Pollution Control Agency (MPCA), responsible for judging Northern

States Power's application to discharge industrial wastes from the Monticello facility.

"One day," Abrahamson recalls, "a member of the Pollution Control Agency came to the university and asked if anyone knew anything about reactors. Apparently the agency had its dander up. Some member had asked NSP about radioactive wastes and the company engineer had replied that it was none of MPCA's business—without bothering to explain that radioactivity was the AEC's responsibility. Well, I had worked on reactor design in the late 1950s at Babcock & Wilcox. One thing led to another. I had to read a lot to catch up with the technology."

Among the documents Abrahamson read were some internal GE memos about the kind of reactor NSP would get at Monticello. Thus, when a GE expert testified—quoting optimistic figures—at a MPCA open hearing in early 1968, Abrahamson rebuked him with GE's own information. "All hell broke loose," Abrahamson says. "No one had ever doubted the veracity of the experts before." Moreover, the incident got his dander up, too.

Together with another University of Minnesota scientist, Abrahamson went on to raise some even more troubling issues at the hearing. Would the discharge of low-level radioactive wastes constitute a threat to marine life in the Mississippi River? The scientists noted that most of the 1.6 million residents of the Twin Cities draw their drinking water from the river a few miles downstream from the Monticello plant's discharge pipes. How much radioactivity would they be taking in with every glass of water? In effect, the focus of discontent with nuclear power plants suddenly shifted from the possibility of major accidents to the reactors' day-to-day operations. Abrahamson's earnest pot shots were shrewdly aimed, and anxious citizens began to organize against the plant.

Northern States Power tried to reassure the people by taking full page ads stating that its nukes "will meet every applicable safety standard established by the AEC" and that the company stood ready to "spend whatever is necessary

to insure the protection of public health and safety." But
how safe were the AEC's standards on radioactivity? Not
having the expertise to answer such a question, the Pollution Control Agency did precisely what any organization
in a quandary would do. In July, 1968, it engaged a con-
sultant, Dr. Ernest C. Tsivoglou of the Georgia Institute of
Technology, who soon got the glib nickname of "the rambling Czech from Georgia Tech."

It is true that Tsivoglou took his time about reaching
any conclusion. As befits a prudent scientist, Tsivoglou
accepted help from members of both sides of the controversy. GE and NSP furnished him with complete data on
the Monticello plant, then helped to formulate a series of
environmental goals and objectives to cut radioactive wastes
as far as technically possible (down to 2 or 3 percent of
AEC limits). Meantime, Abrahamson and other university
scientists had formed the Minnesota Committee for Environmental Information to provide the public with the continuous
technical information which PG & E's opponents at Bodega
Bay had so much trouble in finding. Tsivoglou asked the
scientists to evaluate the risks and benefits of nuclear power
plants and report back to the MPCA. While their resulting
report did not say that the risks outweighed the benefits in
so many words, it raised significant doubts. The report's conclusion says it all: "The clearest fact that emerges from this
discussion is the uncertainty, the experimental nature of the
nuclear program."

That was an understatement. In a letter to *Science* magazine, nuclear critic Sheldon Novick reported that as of
1968, seventeen civilian nuclear power plants had been
completed. Of them, five had been shut down, Novick
wrote, "as impractical or unsafe; a sixth, the Fermi reactor,
was never made to operate properly . . .; a seventh, the
Humbolt plant has operated within allowable radiation
release limits only by reducing power output. The remainder
have had various degrees of difficulty . . ." Once doubts
were planted in such a fertile subject as radioactivity, they
took root and grew. Citizens jumped to obvious conclu-

sions, and the cry went out that low-level radioactivity would disrupt biological rhythms, cause birth defects and increase leukemia deaths in children. Antinuclear songs reverberated in people's minds:

On the mighty Mississippi, near Monticello, Minn.
They're building a nuclear power plant and they're
    committing mortal sin,
They'll contaminate our river with radioactive wastes,
With insidious poison that no one can see or smell or
    taste.

Dr. Tsivoglou then suggested an eminently logical way out of the Minnesota Pollution Control Agency's troubles. In his own final report, released in March, 1969, he changed a key definition. Instead of regarding a standard as a limit below which NSP could dump its low-level radioactive wastes, he urged that the waste discharged from the Monticello plant be held to the lowest possible level. What might that level be? Tsivoglou had NSP's and GE's data to give him the answer. Using the information, he suggested setting new standards—not goals—about fifty times tougher than the AEC's. The MPCA adopted the recommendations in May.

Northern States Power was aghast. "Stated simply," said Bjorn Bjornson, "what was planned as a floor, the Tsivoglou permit made a ceiling." The problem was not really the extra expense that the permit's restrictions would entail, the company insisted. It was that in looking exclusively at the waste aspects of the plant, the new rules neglected other practical considerations. To meet the permit's gaseous release levels, for example, the company would have to shut down the plant with some frequency for fuel changes or modifications. During the shut-downs and start-ups, radioactive emissions would be greater than normal. Moreover, said NSP's president, Robert H. Engels, those fuel changes could expose the plant's personnel to "real and significant increases in radiation doses." As a result, the company criticized the permit as "arbitrary" and "unworkable." Board Chairman Earl Ewald insisted that the chances of anyone's health being damaged by the plant were in the vicinity of one in

100 million. "If this plant would harm anyone," he said, "I would be the first to order it shut down."

Environmentalists, on the other hand, had good reason to praise the strict new standards. Being so much tougher than the AEC's limits, Minnesota's at least began to ease public fears. Moreover, several nuclear critics noted that the AEC had been licensing nuclear power plants as if each were the only one in operation. But it was clear that there were going to be many plants on such major bodies of water as the Mississippi River; Minnesota's standards would lessen the accumulation of low-level wastes flowing downstream. The scientists also warned that radioactivity concentrates in food chains, first in small organisms and then in the fish that eat those organisms. Dr. Donald I. Mount of the National Water Quality Laboratory in Duluth, Minnesota, put it well: "We've got to think of New Orleans."

The AEC kept supplying reassurances. *Our standards take the effect on food chains into account,* AEC scientists said. *The important thing to consider is the concentration and the type of isotope. We don't let any dangerous ones out into the atmosphere. You get more radioactivity in a dentist's office or an airplane than you do from living next door to a nuclear plant.*

But the critics were not easily mollified. Tritium, the long-lived radioactive isotope of hydrogen, would unquestionably leak into the water supply. While the AEC insisted that tritium would not injure human health, independent scientists were not so sure. At worst, tritium might conceivably enter all living organisms with deleterious effects, they said. Krypton, a radioactive gas, might also be distributed throughout the biosphere.

Local citizens sensibly preferred to take the conservative view of minimizing risks. On Mother's Day, 1969, women and children dramatically marched in protest against the plant. "This is getting to be a damned hot political issue," said the citizens group's attorney, Lawrence Cohen. "It's getting to the point where people are going to say, 'We

don't want facts, we just don't want you screwing up the
environment. All we know is that you're doing it, and we
want the right to say you can't'." *You can't,* repeated the
politicians, from Governor Harold LeVander to his state
legislators, who then praised the state standards and roundly
condemned the AEC and NSP. The AEC repled: "Hogwash."

Hogwash? AEC Chairman Glenn Seaborg wrote Governor
LeVander saying Minnesota could not legally set its own
standards for nuclear plants, because Congress gave the
agency sole jurisdiction over atomic development. LeVander
retorted that "Minnesota will not be content to follow a
minimum standard." The state, after all, was only telling the
nuclear industry that it had to live up to a technology that
was better than the standards controlling it. But the AEC
feared a possible precedent, contending that states so lack
the expertise to cope with atomic matters that leaving the
standards to them would lead to "total and utter chaos."
In addition, NSP's Earl Ewald said, "It is impossible for us
to function under two divergent regulatory authorities."

At about this time, Dean Abrahamson recalls, "Things
started slipping away from the real issue of low-level emissions. Even the question of the AEC's credibility was
neglected. The Monticello dispute turned into a battle over
states' rights." That might have been true on the national
scene, but in Minneapolis-St. Paul, citizens did everything
they could to delay granting of all permits to the plant. NSP
began to feel desperate about meeting its commitments to
supply a burgeoning demand for power. In a sure sign that
it was willing to compromise, it voluntarily offered to install
extra environmental safeguards.

Meantime Northern States Power took Minnesota and
its Pollution Control Agency to court to answer just one
question: Does the authority to regulate a nuclear-powered
electric generating plant lie solely with the AEC or with
states as well? Minnesota argued that under the Tenth
Amendment to the U.S. Constitution it had "the power and
duty to regulate and to prevent pollution of its lands, waters
and air above it." The suit was emphatically supported by

several other states, including Vermont, Illinois, Maryland, Texas, Missouri and Michigan. Indeed, there is something faintly ridiculous about the notion that a state cannot set safer rules than the federal government. The basic theory of federalism is that the states are sovereign (except in clearly defined areas like foreign policy) and history has proved that they can serve extremely well as social laboratories for the entire nation. It was California, for example, not the federal government, that pioneered new laws governing auto exhaust emission.

In December, 1970, nevertheless, U. S. District Court Judge Edward J. Devitt ruled that Congress had expressed "an unambiguous mandate to pre-empt the field" for the AEC in a 1959 amendment to the Atomic Energy Act of 1954. Devitt took pains to make clear that he was ruling on a point of law, not on the adequacy or inadequacy of any regulations before him. He did say, however, that "prudence dictates" stiffer standards than the AEC's. Governor LeVander's successor, Wendell Anderson, a Democrat, promptly appealed the decision.

Over the next four months, the last technical and legal objections were resolved at the Monticello plant and the big facility started generating electricity—ten months after it was scheduled to go into commercial operation. The cost of the delay: an estimated $18.9 million in purchases of power from other utilities and use of NSP's older, inefficient plants.

Aside from the fact that interested environmentalists could quite easily delay the operation, if not the actual construction, of a nuke, the Monticello case proved other points. Back in the fall of 1969, the prominence of the case may well have been a contributing factor in the AEC's decision to confront for the first time its critics in the public. The agency sent a group of its members and scientists to Vermont to take part in three open forums. It was as surprising—and inconclusive—a move as if the Department of Defense had debated Dr. Benjamin Spock. Perhaps, too, the Monticello case helped to spur the extensive public hearings on "The Environmental Effects of Producing Electric Power" in late 1969 and early 1970. Held before the Joint Congressional Committee on Atomic Energy, the proceedings fill three thick volumes, which indicates, if nothing else, that the environmental problems of nukes are extensive.

Directly, the Monticello case called national attention to questions about radiation standards. Three other states—Illinois, Vermont and Maryland—eventually followed Minnesota's lead in setting their own tough restrictions on routine radioactive releases from power plants. In total, the attorneys-general or governors of twenty-four states have indicated support of Minnesota's contention before the courts that a state can establish tougher standards than the federal government. Many electric utilities, perhaps anticipating trouble from state governments and environmentalists, have started to submit plans for new reactors complete with added devices to cut radioactive emissions.

In June, 1971, the Atomic Energy Commission took a belated step. It proposed to lower its long-standing and staunchly defended limit on permissible releases of radiation from conventional (light water) reactors by 99 percent. The new rules, the AEC said, would be expressed in reactor design and operating criteria that would hold radioactive releases beyond the plant's site to above five millirems per year above what a nearby resident would get from natural background radiation. This reduction is precisely what Dr.'s Gofman and Tamplin had been urging since 1969, though the AEC insists that it was not responding to their criticism. Rather, the crucial point was whether large new reactors could comply with the lower standards. Apparently, they can. Dr. Gofman hailed the AEC's decision as "a tremendous victory for our position," quickly adding that the nuclear program's problems are still far from solved.

Another thing the Monticello case proved was the effectiveness of collaboration between scientists and citizens. Without Dr. Abrahamson (and his colleagues), the case may never have been so sharply focused on the difficulties of assessing radiation dangers. The bearded professor himself gives high credit to the University of Minnesota. He found important technical support among other faculty members, whether they surfaced in the public eye or not, and also got the implicit blessing of the university administration as well. "Even though many people feel that scientists ought to stay in the laboratory," he says, "my department heads told me to go ahead with the case if I felt that it was important and I wouldn't make any stupid mistakes. Their only restriction was that I never represent myself as speaking for the university."

The case's effect on Northern States Power was far-reaching. If the company had learned something from the dispute over its coal-fired plant on the St. Croix River, it learned even more from the Monticello controversy. And, after what one company official describes as "a lot of soul searching," NSP has come up with a novel procedure for siting future plants. But that is another story.

6. Hot Water

Case studies:
Cayuga Lake, Biscayne Bay,
Lake Michigan.

In its 1970 annual report, President Nixon's Council on Environmental Quality stated that electric power plants account for 81.3 percent of the waste heat being dumped into U. S. waterways. With demand for electricity steadily growing and more nuclear plants being built every year, the council continued, "it is estimated that by 1980 the electric power industry will require the equivalent of 1/5 of the total fresh water run-off of the U. S." As a result, "Many authorities believe that waste heat looms as one of the most serious types of future water pollution."

In the workbook, *Environmental Cost of Electric Power*, Dr. Dean Abrahamson describes the general impact of waste heat:

Some forms of aquatic life die from the increased temperature. Others may become more susceptible to chemical or physical toxins or to organisms causing disease. There is a decrease in spawning success and in the survival of young fish. Normal biological rhythms and migration patterns are disrupted. Prey-predator relationships are disrupted. Oxygen concentrations are decreased at the very times when more oxygen is needed by aquatic life because of increase in temperature. There is an increase in rooted plant growth, leading to decreased river flow rate and increased siltation.

It all sounds very serious, but is it? Asked that question by a visitor, Abrahamson sighed: "By some set of values, the effect may always benefit somebody. A trout stream produces a small amount of high-class fish. Warming a trout stream will lead to downstream changes which might help bass take over. Bass fishermen would not mind. You see, there are trade-offs. At Northern States Power's nuclear installation at Prairie Island, the company is following stringent thermal standards not to dump the hot water into the Mississippi. The basic reason is that the hot water decreases the ability of the river to handle sewage. If NSP did not cool the effluent before letting it into the river, the Minneapolis-St. Paul sewage would have to be upgraded— a very expensive operation."

Because most trade-offs are not so easy to measure, power companies until fairly recently have not bothered to cool their waste heat, understandably disliking to spend money on costly cooling systems that would not return one cool cent on capital investment and would raise the cost of electricity to the consumer. But the dangers of heat, as the Council on Environmental Quality noted, are cumulative, and techniques of cooling are available. One method is to build sizable cooling ponds, where the hot water simply releases its heat over time into the atmosphere. Other techniques accelerate the process. In one, the hot water is sprayed into the air so that the heat will dissipate faster; Commonwealth Edison Company uses such "spray ponds" at its Dresden stations. In another, a "wet" cooling tower mixes the hot water forcefully with air, dispersing the heat mainly by evaporation—which raises other problems.

At the 870-megawatt Besse-Davis reactor, being built on the shores of Lake Erie by Toledo Edison Company and Cleveland Electric Illuminating Company, announcement of a $9-million wet tower system brought mixed reactions.

Citizens were pleased not to add thermal units to the lake's already staggering burden of pollutants. But they had a hard time being enthusiastic about a tower which would loom 450 feet high—taller than even the nearby Commodore Perry Monument—and which might cause mists, fog, or icing. Discharging water vapor into the air instead of heated water into the lake, one critic said, "is only trading off one environmental insult for another."

Technically, the best answer of all is to use a "dry" cooling tower which works like a giant automobile radiator. Yet even this solution would not only be sure to offend esthetic sensibilities, but also to cost so many millions of dollars, that no electric utility in the United States has yet built one.

Two overriding thermal problems have confronted environmentalists combatting hot water. One was defined in a statement by Florida's Governor Claude Kirk during the first federal-state "conference" on thermal pollution: "I wish to point out to the participants and to the nation the utter foolishness of allowing the Atomic Energy Commission the right to grant construction permits for . . . [nuclear powered electric generating plants] without paying any attention to the ecological impact of their future operation." Even though now required by the National Environmental Policy Act to file detailed statements describing the impact of a power plant on the environment, the AEC has steadfastly refused to claim any jurisdiction over thermal pollution. Instead, the burden falls on individual states with their differing water quality laws. Unfortunately, the result has been the kind of lax enforcement that has driven environmentalists into their own heated and intransigent positions.

The other immense problem is proof of damage. Anyone who thinks about the problem of thermal pollution in general is certain to recognize the need for cooling all power plants' waste heat. Who wants the hot water eventually to run out of his cold water tap, or blue-green slime to clog his favorite fishing hole? What is much less certain is how to judge the situation at specific power plant sites where realistic decisions must be made. Every ecological situation is different and, given the limited facts known about each, trying to prove that hot water discharges are harmful is like trying to prove that cigarettes cause cancer. At first glance, it seems almost impossible to pin down— at least before the damage occurs. But conservationists, aided by concerned scientists and tough lawyers, have found unusual and potent ways of making the impossible possible.

Cayuga Lake: Setting a Pattern

Cayuga, largest of the Finger Lakes—38 miles long and about 1½ miles wide—has unique characteristics. Its "flushing time" (the time it would take a drop of water to move from one end of the lake to an outlet at the other end) is nine and one-half years. With cold, deep water (mean depth: 179 feet), Cayuga is what limnologists call a "thermally stratified" lake; between May and November, warmer water forms a thick upper layer that never mixes with the colder water below.

Onto this lake intruded New York State Electric & Gas Company (NYSE&G) with plans for its 830-megawatt "Bell" reactor at Lansing. The nuke would draw cooling water from the chilly (forty-five degree) bottom layer, send it through the reactor's condensers, and discharge it at about sixty-five to seventy degrees into the warmer surface layer. This process would occur continuously at a rate of about 500,000 gallons a minute.

Typically, NYSE&G did not breathe a word about its plans until June, 1967, when it had acquired options on its site and conducted preliminary surveys—none of which included ecological studies. Typically too, the news was greeted with disinterest by most residents and with enthusiasm by county officials who welcomed the thought of a hefty increase in the local tax base. In fact, it seems extremely improbable that the proposed Bell reactor would have generated a kilowatt of controversy had not a group of scientists at Cornell University, twelve miles away from the site, been interested in the plant's impact on the lake. In June, 1968, the group, led by Alfred W. Eipper, an associate professor of fishery biology, published a booklet titled *Thermal Pollution of Cayuga Lake by a Proposed Power Plant,* known by the less ominous name of the Eipper Report.

The scientists warned that NYSE&G's plans would speed up the lake's aging process—the same eutrophication that has so harmed Lake Erie—by an unknown rate. How? By dumping waste heat into Cayuga's upper layer, thermal stratification would occur earlier in the season and last longer than ever before. Overenriched and warmed, aquatic animals and plants would proliferate. In particular, the scientists mentioned a single-celled alga which eventually would give the water "a diluted pea-soup appearance." The reactor's eventual impact would therefore be to diminish the value of Cayuga's waters for recreation or as habitat for such desirable fish as lake trout.

"These are not assumptions, but simple known facts," Eipper wrote in the *Ithaca Journal.* Even so, he mentioned, it was up to NYSE&G to prove that the plant posed no threat to the lake. The scientists urged the company to build cooling towers to prevent the problems from ever occurring. They approvingly cited a decision taken by the Vermont Yankee Nuclear Power Corporation to install cooling towers costing $6.5 million at its Vernon, Vermont, reactor. Annual operation and maintenance of those towers, the Eipper Report noted, would amount to $900,000, which would be passed along to the customers in a 1 percent increase in the cost of electricity.

NYSE&G was not impressed. Cooling towers would be expensive not only to purchase but to build on the company's hillside site. Moreover, they would cause a decrease in the plant's efficiency. In total, the utility said, indulging in industrial hyperbole, the towers would cost $21.3 million to install plus an annual $2.4 million to operate. A much cheaper alternative would be to study whether the Eipper

Report's dire conclusions were true. NYSE&G, accordingly, decided to spend $500,000 on research by independent scientists at Cornell, its subsidiary Aeronautical Lab, and the State University of New York at Buffalo. All the while, site preparation for the reactor continued.

Not surprisingly, the new research eventually showed that the Eipper Report may—or may not—have overstated the case. The reports all used different models, assumptions, and interpretations of past data. "Few of the individuals or groups," Eipper later wrote in *Science* magazine, "seem to have been concerned with seriously challenging the validity of estimates put forward by others." He did applaud, however, the innovative thinking that grew out of the controversy. One physicist, for example, suggested that the plant could help to reverse eutrophication already underway, Eipper said, "by using some of the generated electricity to remove nutrients from the water in its passage through the cooling cycle. . . . Other scientists proposed an ingenious scheme for building a pumped storage cooling pond several hundred feet above the lakeside plant site. Company spokesmen said this scheme was not economically feasible."

The dispute was never resolved. In September, 1968, concerned residents of the area banded together to form the Citizens Committee to Save Cayuga Lake (CSCL), in effect the godfather of all citizen-scientist coalitions. Its position was not to oppose nuclear power per se but to try to get NYSE&G to protect the environment adequately. Dorothy Nelkin in *Nuclear Power and Its Critics* (Cornell University Press) attributes CSCL's success mainly to the skill of its executive director, a research associate in Soviet studies at Cornell, David D. Comey.

Comey perfected the tactics that were to be widely copied elsewhere in other battles against nuclear plants. Backed by a solid core of Cornell scientists, he publicized for CSCL the potential dangers of the proposed plant—not only thermal but also radiation pollution. The local newspapers found CSCL's constant stream of press releases irresistible, and topped them with such headlines as "Cayuga Lake

Shouldn't Look Like Diluted 'Pea Soup.' " Comey himself was free to move quickly without consulting the group's membership of 800. "Prompt and open responses were made to public inquiries," Dorothy Nelkin writes. "In contrast, the NYSE&G was slow to release information, was most often inaccessible to the press, and was cautious if not defensive regarding public controversy." As a result, the utility lost credibility in the eyes of the community.

On the other hand, no agency seemed responsible for defending the environment. The AEC refused to consider any of the nuclear plant's effects save radiation. The federal government has no jurisdiction over intrastate waters like Cayuga Lake. Even the state government did not help; the agency empowered to issue a permit for the plant to discharge hot water, the state Health Department, got into considerable hot water itself for being as concerned with industrial development as with pollution. Alarmed at the evident weakness in state procedures, one New York legislator asked Governor Nelson Rockefeller to block construction of the Bell reactor. Other politicians introduced remedial bills in the 1969 state legislature. Then, on April 11, 1969, NYSE&G stopped immediate controversy by announcing postponement of its plans for the Bell reactor pending "additional research on cooling systems for thermal discharge from the plant and for consideration of the economic effects of such systems." The research reports were finished in 1969, but as already noted, did not end questions about the thermal issue.

Testifying before the Joint Committee on Atomic Energy in 1970, David Comey warned that the citizens group is ready to oppose the company if it simply repeats its earlier proposal. "We feel we have a convincing case for adding safeguards to the present design of Bell Station," he said. "We have tried to be as responsible in handling these issues as we know how." Senator Edmund Muskie, speaking specifically of thermal pollution, said it better. "You've got to take the point of view that if we don't know enough, we don't know enough to permit the discharge."

Biscayne Bay: Opening a Pandora's Box

Biscayne Bay on the east coast of southern Florida is as unlike Cayuga Lake as a puddle from a well. Where Cayuga is deep and cold, Biscayne Bay averages only seven feet in depth and is always tepid. Most of its 105 square miles are protected from the Atlantic by Key Largo and a succession of other smaller keys. It teems with marine life and is in many respects so unique that Congress in 1968 included a major part of the bay in the Biscayne National Monument. The designation: "To preserve and protect for the education, inspiration, recreation and enjoyment of future generations of Americans a rare combination of terrestrial, marine and amphibious life in a typical setting of great beauty."

Poking into the bay like a big toe, twenty-five miles south of Miami, is a stubby Dade County peninsula called Turkey Point. Whether it was named after the water turkey that nests there or for the shape of the terrain is uncertain. In any case, it became a battlefield.

In 1964, officials of the Florida Power & Light Company (FPL), fresh from squabbles with the residential neighbors of its Cutler plant in south Dade County, found Turkey Point a most enticing place. Other people at that time would have described it as desolate, a sunbaked mangrove swamp awash at high tide with brackish waters. But because it was secluded—and likely to remain so—the company decided that Turkey Point could serve as the location for a complex of generating stations consisting first of twin oil-fired plants and later of two nuclear reactors. FPL bought 1,800 acres of land, obtained permits from the county and AEC, and by 1967 had its two oil-fired facilities sending 854 megawatts of electricity to its consumers. In the process, the utility proudly transformed much of Turkey Point into a park with picnic area, archery range and swimming lake. Reflecting the conservation interests of FPL's Chairman McGregor Smith, a self-made millionaire, another 1,500 acres were reserved as a wildlife sanctuary, home for crocodiles, raccoons, otters, and hundreds of species of wild birds.

Instead of reaping continuing praise for creating what one newspaper called "a model of partnership between industry and nature," FPL quickly ran into trouble. It had not foreseen the thermal problem. Its oil-fired units each minute spewed 275,000 gallons of hot water into the bay, and while this amounted to just a drop in the waters, company officials had cause to worry about the future. The tides usually do not flush Biscayne Bay well. Instead they often merely slosh its waters around like waves in a bathtub. Because waste heat from the plant sometimes remained near the shoreline, it might once again be sucked into the cooling system and discharged even hotter than before. What would happen when the company built its two nuclear reactors at Turkey Point? If the natural cooling waters were too hot to cool the reactors' condensers, the units would have to shut down.

Conservationists—including local chapters of the Izaak Walton League and the Audubon Society—saw the nukes in another light. The heated water from the oil-fired units, they said, was already creating havoc in Biscayne Bay. Generating 1,520 megawatts and discharging 1.8 million gallons a minute, the nuclear units almost certainly would make a "wasteland" in the waters. As evidence, a study by the Hoover Foundation pointed out that climatologically Biscayne Bay rests "squarely" on the line that separates the tropics, where it never freezes, from the subtropics, where it seldom freezes. Aquatic and marine life change radically in the area of the bay, the report continued, so the location of the nuclear facility was critical. Unless the thermal discharges never exceeded ninety-two degrees, marine life would be killed, perhaps changing the ecology of the national monument. In other words, Turkey Point was precisely the wrong place for the nuke.

To emphasize that point the conservationist groups produced high-level photographs of the extent of damage done by the existing generating units at an April 1969 hearing on the controversy before the Senate Subcommittee on Water

Pollution. Yet, they were voices crying in a watery wilderness, not only unheeded but contested.

"The truth of the matter is that practically nothing is known about the temperature tolerance of species that inhabit southern Florida," FPL Chairman Smith told a reporter. Smith repeated this argument to the Senate subcommittee, adding that hot water might actually benefit the fish, while cold water kills them. He added:

> We should seriously object to any unnecessary and additional burden placed on nuclear power. We should be able to compete with the rest of the country by using our coastline as a natural resource. The three million Floridians served by FPL have an important stake in the use and continued development of atomic power and they are entitled to the proper use of their bay the same as boaters and others, without any penalty or unnecessary charges being placed on them.

Conservationists were again disappointed at a later hearing by the President's Advisory Committee on Water Pollution, despite clear proof of thermal troubles. In June, 1969, the oil-fired plant emitted 103-degree water one day and great quantities of fish turned belly up and died. Some 670 acres of bay bottom were described as "scoured." The evidence was damning.

To be sure, Florida Power & Light was already worrying about hot water, if not the fish. The company had its public image to consider and, more important, it had to make sure that the nukes would get cool water from the bay. After investigating various alternatives, the company concluded that cooling towers would not help, since they would emit salt spray which might waft onto nearby farms. Instead, the company chose to build an $8-million cooling canal from the nuclear site six miles through mangrove swamp to Card Sound, a much smaller body of water just south of Biscayne Bay. Local and state officials agreed.

Predictably, the decision appalled conservationists. The canal would not cool the heated water enough to spare the marine life in the sound, they charged, appealing to the state for help. Because Governor Claude Kirk was not sure that Florida had jurisdiction over a dispute involving interstate waters, he invited the U. S. Department of Interior in December, 1969, to call the first federal-state conference on thermal pollution, "in order that we may preserve the unique environment of Biscayne Bay and adjacent bodies of water." A date for the conference was set in February, 1970.

In helpless outrage, James F. Redford, the president of the Mangrove chapter of the Izaak Walton League, told the Joint Congressional Committee on Atomic Energy what was going on in Florida.

Neighboring land has already been condemned for the [canal] by the circuit court of Dade County, and construction is due to begin [on] February 1, despite the fact that the enforcement conference is called for the 24th. . . . [Florida Power & Light contended it] cannot stop digging the canal even though they have not the permits to dig in the tidal lands which they would have to get from the Army Corps of Engineers, the county and state. They say they will take the chance, the three or four weeks they have to wait will make a great deal of difference.

Hopes for a definitive treatment of thermal pollution problems evaporated when the conference began. Murray Stein of the Federal Water Quality Administration read a statement warning that the Interior Department "will request the U. S. Justice Department to seek appropriate remedies to protect the Biscayne Bay National Monument, including court action if necessary." He then returned to his seat to act as chairman of the conference—that is, as both prosecutor and judge. One Miami paper was quick to charge in an editorial: "In another place in another time . . . this might have been called a kangaroo court. Even before FPL had an opportunity to present scientific witness on its behalf, the company was ordered to desist from building [its] cooling canal."

In time, of course, all participants had their say. The

feds charged that "severe damage has already occurred to the aquatic plant and animal population of lower Biscayne Bay due to the heated effluent from the Turkey Point plant." Other witnesses argued that hot water cannot be proved to have harmed fish. A power company executive emphasized that "anything that slows down this project threatens a power shortage in June of next year." The conference ended with the FWQA setting a ninety-degree maximum on heated discharges, though Dade County officials had set the limit at ninety-five degrees. It was, reported the *Washington Post,* "the kind of rambling town meeting that young people dismiss these days as empty rhetoric."

"We did not do too well in Miami," Interior Department officials conceded. Even so, they knew the plant's effluents would undeniably affect Card Sound. Stein put it this way: "We found that the waters of the sound are ecologically as perfect as nature can make. These waters are unspoiled by man-made pollution despite the proximity of man's presence. Therefore the user must protect the waters." What Stein saw as the greatest danger was the probability that heat would "cook" minute marine life drawn with the cooling water through the nuke's condensers. And according to federal scientists' calculations, the plant, when completed, would every month cycle a volume of water equivalent to the natural content of Biscayne Bay and send it, boiled aquatic life and all, into Card Sound. "My judgment," said Stein, "is that if we've got an ecological balance that took thousands of years to produce, you're going to change it in the cycling process. You really don't know what's going to happen. You open a Pandora's box."

The U. S. Justice Department repeated much of this argument in March, 1970, when it brought suit against FPL, seeking an injunction against alleged present and future ecological disturbances because of the plant's operation. This injunction was denied a month later by the Federal District Court, which concluded that Turkey Point's two fossil-fired plants could not be proven to cause irreparable damage. The case has nonetheless remained before the court on other grounds, including the future effects of hot water poured out by nukes. Under the Rivers & Harbors Act of 1899, moreover, discharge of any refuse—including, presumably, hot water—into navigable waters is forbidden. But what should have been the definitive case in thermal pollution was settled out of court in late 1971. FPL agreed to drop its canal scheme and build instead a 4,000-acre, closed system cooling pond. The lesson? Only that siting big power plants on Florida's ecologically fragile coastline makes little environmental or business sense.

Lake Michigan: Victory at Last

Romney Wheeler, a vice-president of Consumers Power Company (CP), is a tall, courtly man who wears respectability as easily as his dark pin-striped suit. Carefully choosing his words, he draws the moral from his company's experience in 1970-71 with its $125-million reactor at Palisades, Michigan:

It is possible for a small determined group to impose the tactics of delay to cause a financial hemorrhage, so that an electric utility is forced by two overriding considerations to do what the environmentalists want it to do. The first is the need to bring generating capacity into service; Consumers Power had 20 percent of its total capacity tied up for nine months. The second is the need to stop the hemorrhage. Delay was costing the company about $1 million a month, comprised of the continuing cost of capital and the need to buy power elsewhere to serve our customers.

Tyson Cross, CP's director of public information, sees a somewhat tarnished silver lining in the experience:

There is now a backlash against so-called environmentalists, even from young people. CP people are all over the northern part of Michigan and are easily accessible. They're being told that the Palisades controversy is a crime, the consequences of an emotional outpouring by a small group of people. They're asking

"What's this country coming to when an insignificant minority can tyrannize the majority?"

The Palisades reactor is located on the shores of Lake Michigan, about thirty-five miles due west of Kalamazoo. Its early operation was vital to Consumers Power's operations, whose service area includes Michigan's entire lower peninsula. By 1970, the company knew, 1.1 million customers would demand 3,685 megawatts of power. Without the new 700-megawatt plant, CP could generate only 3,500 megawatts. Still, the company did not expect any significant opposition. Its schedule for the new reactor ended on this confident listing: "May 1970—commercial operation."

When the first AEC hearings on a construction permit were held in 1966, Romney Wheeler recalls, "everybody in Cobo township was there; they served cookies and coffee. No one objected to the reactor." But when the AEC held hearings in June, 1970, to permit low-level testing of the reactor, there were objectors who plainly doubted CP's often stated promise that "we will not knowingly change the ecology of Lake Michigan." One was Ron McCandlis, twenty-six, a fisherman representing the Michigan Steelhead and Salmon Fishermen's Association. Feeling threatened by the thermal effects of the plant on Lake Michigan, he spoke of his fears on his weekly fishing radio report. In four weeks, McCandlis collected 40,000 signatures on a petition against the plant. With him was the veteran of Cayuga Lake's controversy, David D. Comey, enticed from Ithaca to Chicago to join a group called Businessmen for the Public Interest (BPI). Noted for its backing of Ralph Nader (the money came mainly from the heir to the Midas muffler fortune), BPI wanted to get involved in the environmental field and chose power as one platform. What most bothered these men was the possibility that nuclear discharges of hot water would upset the ecology of Lake Michigan, already polluted by sewage and industrial wastes.

As Romney Wheeler describes it, the most interesting opponent was Myron Cherry, "a spectacular, kaleidoscopic lawyer with unorthodox tactics. He opened every avenue of delay through cross-questioning." And delay was what Consumers Power could not afford.

Mike Cherry was an antitrust lawyer in Chicago when he first got involved in the dispute. One of his firm's senior partners, an avid boater, was sailing in Lake Michigan when he almost ran into some old ships that Consumers Power had sunk to serve as breakwaters around the Palisades reactor. He angrily called to ask what the company was doing and was told, Cherry remembers, "something like 'It's a secret government project.'" This reply so enraged the partner that he asked Mike Cherry to go to the hearings and give the utility "a little trouble for a couple of days." Cherry's life and the electric utility business have never been the same since. Indeed, Cherry might well occupy a pivotal point in antinuclear disputes: the replacement of technicians, such as those behind the Cayuga dispute, with lawyers.

Bushy haired and quick witted, Cherry had been trained for corporate work. That background gave him a useful perspective. "I saw that under administrative law, it does not pay to argue my expert against your expert. The Gofman-Tamplin approach is not the way to try a national law suit," he says. "The case was really not about the plant but about AEC procedures. I started on the assumption that the AEC was legally wrong on thermal pollution. The commission took the position that it had no jurisdiction over thermal effects. . . . Yet its mandate is to regulate atomic energy. There are two forms of energy involved here, radioactivity and heat. Since the AEC had to regulate heat inside a nuclear plant, it obviously should regulate it outside the plant, too." Cherry's argument was fruitless, but it was innovative and brash enough to surprise the opposing lawyers—quite a change from the usual interveners' humdrum arguments.

Cherry also had three tactical advantages. One was that the chairman of the Atomic Safety and Licensing Board, Samuel Jensch, had been for years disturbed by the way the AEC gave out licenses; he wanted the procedures put to the acid test by good trial lawyers, and Cherry was happy to oblige. Cherry and his assistants were also willing to work all night, if need be, to prepare legal briefs. In fact, Cherry drilled his team as if it were going to the Rose Bowl. He instituted "hate sessions," and cut out meals to keep assistants fit and angry. In contrast, Consumers Power and the AEC's regulatory staff staidly quit work at 5 p.m. As a result, the interveners usually were able to answer Jensch's questions within tight time limits while their opponents often could not.

As in all such hearings, the controversy swirled around several subjects besides heat pollution. Radiation, for instance. To all intents and purposes, the Palisades reactor was as safe as could then be made: radioactive discharges would average less than 2 percent of AEC standards. But the fishermen—joined by the Sierra Club, Michigan Lakes and Streams Association, Concerned Petitioning Citizens, and Thermal Ecology Must Be Preserved (TEMP)—nonetheless questioned the "yearly average" method by which the AEC measures radiation. They believed that this practice would allow CP to discharge more than a safe amount during certain months of the year, but still be below the allowed limit by shutting off the reactor at other times. More important, they did not want the Palisades plant to set any precedent, for there were nine other nuclear plants being built around Lake Michigan and two more planned. In other words, Consumers Power just happened to be unlucky for being first; the controversy really centered on the plethora of nukes rimming the lake.

"Most of the danger comes from heat, not radioactivity," Cherry says. "When the other plants are in operation, between 7 and 10 billion gallons of heated water would be poured into the lake every day." McCandlis adds: "Most of the people with houses around the lake are worried about the effects the warm water will have on erosion. The shoreline is receding every year and with hot water being pumped continuously into the lake, the erosion will last all year instead of nine months."

Cherry filed a suit on TEMP's behalf in the U. S. District Court of Appeals to try to force the AEC to consider thermal pollution effects. The court ruled against TEMP but added: "If the Commission persists in excluding such evidence, it is courting the possibility that if error is found a court will reverse the final order, condemn proceedings as so much waste motion, and order that the proceedings be conducted over again in a way that realistically permits *de novo* consideration of the tendered evidence." Cherry thinks that is a fine precedent for future reference.

As approved by the state, the Palisades plant would pour into the lake 368,000 gallons a minute. Though the water would be heated by twenty-eight degrees, Consumers Power insisted it would do no harm. "It's like taking a medicine dropper and emptying its contents into a bathtub over twenty-four hours," said Romney Wheeler. The company therefore saw cooling towers as an unnecessary burden on its customers. Moreover the company had some scientific evidence to back its position. Oceanographer John C. Ayres, who had studied Lake Michigan for eleven years, reported: "We have not yet been able to find evidence of adverse effects of generating plant cooling water upon the Great Lakes aquatic ecology." Since virtually all other researchers in the area agreed, Consumers Power challenged the interveners to produce contradictory evidence, even by one scientist.

That was all Cherry needed: "Most scientists refused to show up, because they were not sure of the long-term effects of thermal pollution. But I learned about Dr. John Bardach, an elderly Austrian who had taught at the University of Michigan. Two and a half years earlier he had advised CP not to build its plant on that particular part of the shoreline because the lake was undergoing rapid eutrophication there. I bought a case of Koenigsberg beer and some Viennese sausage and went to see him. Two or three hours later, he said he felt guilty at not speaking out, that the shoreline would be damaged and that more plants would destroy the lake."

Cherry convinced Dr. Bardach to testify at an "enforcement conference" on Lake Michigan's problems held in the early spring of 1971 by the federal government and the states of Michigan, Illinois, Indiana and Wisconsin. "The Federal Water Quality Administration took Bardach's word," Cherry says. "They issued a new standard requiring some sort of closed cooling system unless the utilities can prove that there won't be any harm to the lake. Obviously no one can say what effects thermal pollution might have, but the burden of proof is now switched from citizens to power companies."

William D. Ruckelshaus, administrator of the U. S. Environmental Protection Agency, was a bit more cautious. He contended that while more research is needed on thermal pollution, there is already enough evidence of serious damage to water quality to justify federal insistence that the power companies take precautions to prevent further degradation. The states all fell in line, adopting the new standards, though Illinois refused to make Commonwealth Edison install cooling towers at its Zion plant. As a footnote to the conference, the Indiana & Michigan Electric Company sued Ruckelshaus in July, 1971, asking the court to enjoin the agency from forcing Michigan to accept the requirements. The attempt is to get EPA to fix firm standards on which the utilities can base their plans.

But the tactics of delay paid off. Consumers Power decided to come to terms with the interveners. The conservation groups drove a very tough bargain, stipulating that the company install a "zero radway system" within two years to bring radioactive emissions to an absolute minimum. CP would also have to supply written reports on the latest available technology for this purpose. In addition, the environmentalists insisted on cooling towers to prevent thermal pollution, giving the company three years to put in natural draft towers or four years to build mechanical draft towers. The settlement, which also included provisions for matters involving nuclear safety, would be enforced by the AEC—which meant that the commission would for the first time be regulating thermal as well as radioactive emissions.

Consumers Power sees the conservationists' victory as a blow both to the scientific approach (no ironclad proof that hot water harms the lake) and to the customer's pocket-book. "The settlement will cost between $12 and $15 million for cooling towers and devices to reduce radioactivity," says Romney Wheeler. "It will cost another $2 million in operating and capital charges on the equipment. To install the cooling towers on a completed plant will also reduce the facility's efficiency by forty megawatts. We entered into the agreement only to allow the plant to start operations— not because the antipollution devices are needed. Unfortunately, the added costs will have to be paid by the consumer on his electric bill."

That is not the point, replies Cherry. "The industry has dumped its wastes into the environment for fifty years," he says. "Why should a utility use Lake Michigan as a heat sink? It's time they stopped taking a robber-baron approach to consumer safety. All our prior efforts to get cooperation from the AEC have been fruitless. This case changes the ground rules, that's all."

But that's a lot.

7. Planning with the People

Case study:
Berkshire-Litchfield.

A good deal of industry's difficulty in the siting of power plants can be traced directly to its failure to keep the public informed. Indeed, no less an authority than Consolidated Edison Company Chairman Charles Luce once said that prior disclosure of construction plans would help to eliminate environmental objections to new plants. Luce might have added, of course, that prior disclosure could also "eliminate" some *plants* as well. Still, his point had validity for an industry whose traditional closed-door planning process leads it increasingly into later confrontations with aroused citizens. As the President's Office of Science and Technology noted in 1970: "We need comprehensive, coordinated, timely reviews by all appropriate government and interested private groups of the environmental implications of the utilities' plans early in the planning process."

To most of the industry, following that kind of advice is just asking for more trouble. After all, hasn't it always been the utilities' job—not the public's—to choose sites for new plants, and isn't a power executive's lot hard enough without inviting raving know-nothings to look over his shoulder? But recently, two big electric companies did surrender at least part of the unilateral decision-making process to develop what they called "open planning." And as industry watched, these companies—Northern States Power and Northeast Utilities—achieved startlingly dissimilar results.

Roland W. Comstock is a Young Turk at Northern States Power. Bright, cool and articulate, he rose to prominence during the Monticello controversy and now is the company's director of environmental affairs, *i.e.,* the front man in dealing with a now alert public. Partly at his urging, NSP broke industry tradition in December, 1969, by announcing it would disclose its fifteen-year construction program and its intention to promote public discussion on the location of its next plants and transmission lines. By March, 1970, the company had formed a forty-man "task force," including representatives from state and regional government plus the groups that had been NSP's severest critics.

"Not one group refused to participate," Comstock says, "although many were very hesitant, fearing all of this was just another public relations façade and that they would be used by the company to their disadvantage." For a while, meetings of the task force were conducted in an atmosphere of suspicion and hostility, and NSP management wondered if their bold program would be futile, ridiculous, masochistic. But the experiment continued, with top officers dropping in on task force meetings (to indicate that the company was serious) and with outside consultants doing most of the initial briefing on the utility business (to enhance that most elusive quality of credibility).

"About the sixth week, something very significant happened," says Comstock. "The group itself turned upon one of the most outspoken critics and in effect told him to shut up, that they felt they had a chance to do something constructive. From that point on, the dynamics of the group began to change." Given a choice of four different sites for the next NSP plant, the task force worked hard before selecting one that the company had already said it did not favor. Yet NSP swallowed its independence and followed the group's recommendation. As a result, Comstock says, "It looks as if NSP will be able to install a generating station without a public confrontation for the first time in over a decade."

A signal achievement? Perhaps. But the task force feels it is operating within very tight parameters. William Zimmermann, a physics professor at the University of Minnesota and the group's leader, explains that what many members of the task force crave is the chance to look into broader issues, such as whether new plants should be sited in precious river valleys, or how the company might best use its advertising to advise the public on conservation of electricity. Zimmermann says the group has not been particularly successful in such areas. And he feels morale among the members is getting low because NSP's top management, Rollie Comstock included, seems increasingly disinterested in the experiment. "Since our members run the risk of being used, they should feel the gratification that they're being heard," says Zimmermann. He nonetheless thinks that the open planning experiment has value and should continue—but only if it can accomplish some demonstrable good.

The other open planning experiment risked much more. Northeast Utilities (NU), a giant holding company of Connecticut and Massachusetts utilities, is run by Lelan F. Sillin. A big man with lofty ideals, he admits he has practical problems. "Our assignment is to fulfill power needs, and New England's power needs are growing," he says. "How we effectively meet the public interest—that is, how we provide power while protecting the environment—is in the end a matter of judgment . . . for there are no pragmatic criteria. No one needs any kind of expertise to see the environmental effects of power plants; the technology available *does* have an impact on the environment. What are we prepared to pay in an environmental as opposed to an economic sense?"

To find the answer, Sillin took the question to the people in 1970. Specifically at issue was a proposal for a gigantic pumped storage facility (like the one planned for Storm King) somewhere in the Berkshire Mountains along the Connecticut-Massachusetts state line. Two sites were offered for the consideration of what NU hoped would be representative of the public—a group of open planners—residents working with conservation organizations and state and regional agencies. "We realized that the people of the area have a direct interest in the project," says Sillin, "but so do the people of the region." The problem: to determine where a pumped storage plant should be sited—if at all.

Although the company owned no land in the target areas and sought no options, few people believed NU was not devising some devious utility trick. Why would a company come out into the open when it could use established, behind-the-scenes procedures to ensure approval of the project? Why would the company choose alternate sites for study on opposite sides of a state line if not to divide the opposition? "Our first disappointment was not achieving greater recognition and support of what we were trying to do," Sillin says. "People in our cynical society look for angles."

After making preliminary studies, NU's engineers decided in April, 1971, that the site in Connecticut was the superior of the two alternatives. A 2,000-megawatt pumped storage plant could be built slightly less expensively there ($273.3 million $v.$ $278.6 million), would take less land for reservoirs (about 1,500 $v.$ 2,750 acres) and would not inflict so obvious a change on the landscape. These conclusions were duly made public on the theory that the better-informed concerned citizens are, the better choices they can make.

Meantime, the enormity of the project had appalled many people in the affected area. Lincoln Foster, a retired schoolteacher, is happiest tending his renowned rock garden near Canaan, Connecticut, right where one reservoir might be. When he heard of NU's plans in 1970, he wasted no time in organizing opposition. "I have enough imagination to know what it might be to be submerged," he says. "There are a lot of influential people in this corner of Connecticut who don't want the high valleys flooded either." The result was the Berkshire-Litchfield Environmental Conservation Council (BLECC).

"Our position," says Foster, "is that we do not want to push the plant out of this location to another. We don't want a pumped storage plant anywhere. It is an extravagant use of land and water." Moreover, he says, there are other options: "In New England, it just so happens that the topography suits pumped storage. Other places meet the problem of providing peak-time power with combustion engines."

Difficult as it might seem to fight a project that was only an idea, BLECC girded for combat immediately. In July, 1970, it petitioned the Federal Power Commission not to grant to Northeast Utilities permits to make "preliminary" studies. The petition failed. Foster remembers the engineers as "polite men." But bulldozers soon growled through the woods and the consequent silt made his backyard stream "flow like peanut butter." Since then, BLECC has maintained its original position: that pumped storage is an inefficient and wasteful technology, and that there are better alternatives available, including conservation of energy wherever possible. BLECC officials say they have nothing against open planning *per se,* though they think that their community was brought into the process very late indeed—after the decision to locate the plant in the area had been taken. The project still pends.

In 1970 Sillin embarked on what he calls "our second experiment." One company in NU's family, Connecticut Power & Light, wanted to build a seventy-five-mile-long transmission line connecting the southwestern corner of Connecticut to the New England power grid by 1976. Like all transmission lines, this one would take a lot of land— the rule of thumb is 100 acres per mile of line. Moreover, it would be unsightly. To bury the line, however, would cost $130 million, while stringing it overhead would cost $10 million (the power company's total revenues in 1969 were $150 million). Foreseeing problems, company engineers carefully chose a general route which avoided as many populated areas as possible. The trade-off, of course, was that the line would slash across unspoiled landscapes.

Once again, NU voluntarily took its general plan before the public rather than follow the industry's usual procedure of working through bureaucratic channels and then simply taking the land it needed under eminent domain. "We thought we could present our findings and our judgment," says Sillin. "After we heard public response, we would make changes, revisions and redefine a specific right of way. Instead, the people saw our plan and accused us of wanting to acquire a mile-wide swath through the state. We had bought no land or options."

The company was not only rebuffed; it was devastated. The project's opponents swarmed to open hearings before Connecticut's Public Utilities Commission. They included many of the area's most illustrious residents: William Styron, Vladimir Horowitz, Richard Widmark, Robert Anderson and Arthur Miller—all represented by David Sive, a top conservation lawyer. Highlight of one session was Arthur Miller's statement, an eloquent view of the dilemmas of power:

> I am sure that the businessmen and engineers in the power industry who have designed this project believe that it represents progress. Progress not only for the power business but for the people of this state as well. I am equally sure that none of these men is against beauty. So the question, I think, is how much landscape you are ready to destroy for how much progress . . .
>
> I like my comfort. I remember stoking the coal furnace, and I'd much rather flick a switch to heat the house. I remember the iceman tracking through the kitchen and I'd much rather have an electric refrigerator. I am not here simply to convince people to go back to the simple life. I believe in progress if only because it leaves people time to feed not only their mouths but perhaps their souls.
>
> But I have come to understand that as with anything else in this life, you pay a price for everything. And I

want to ask the utility industry and the state officers involved in this project whether they have studied the dimensions of the price we shall have to pay for this power line project . . .

Certainly the cost of pylons and cables and the rest were calculated, but has anyone figured in the value of any land in sight of that overhead screen of wires? We do not mine coal in Connecticut, or gold or silver. One of our realest and most valuable resources is that intangible feeling of well-being as we look out on unde-filed woodland, the forest unmarked by steel girders. There are scores in towns along the pathway of this project whose basic resource is purely and simply the view, townships populated by families who have paid their good money for a piece of land where they can walk with a bit of beauty . . .

I would like to say to the public utility industry that it is your responsibility now to come forward with alternatives to this project . . . And if you say that research will take years, the only intelligent answer must be that it will be worth years . . . It is bad enough to see the ruin of beauty when the life of the people makes it necessary, but it is unpardonable when it is done because not enough time and money and passion went into its avoidance . . .

So fierce was this controversy that a new state law was passed to establish a Utilities Power Facilities Evaluation Council to oversee the siting of all sizable power plants and transmission lines. "It is the toughest siting authority in the nation," says Sillin, believing that the new rules may add as much as three and a half years to the construction of any new power project. "We know we need that line; we are going to have to have transmission in that area."

In light of Northeast Utilities' experience, it is no wonder that the power industry looks on open planning as "the path to disaster." Sillin is not convinced. "When I talk about open planning I do not expect everybody to say it's just great. But there has to be a certain kind of discipline and order, and respect for an honest answer. Now that the environmental problems have been identified, we have to make the system work. I think, short term, that we have taken our lickings. But long term, we will build a sense of credibility and honesty that is absolutely fundamental to the future of this country."

Sillin is right, but he and other open planners need help —from the legislative branch of government (of the many bills before Congress to ease siting problems of power facilities, none has passed), from the industry itself, and most of all, from the people. They must choose between more electricity and less damage to the environment of their own backyards. And they must let that choice be known.

8. Coming Battles

In a recent study of future demand for electricity, California Institute of Technology's Environmental Quality Laboratory assumed the most conservative conditions possible—near-zero population growth and a 50-percent cut in both per capita affluence and per capita consumption of electricity. Even in the case of such unlikely events, the study projects "a threefold increase in electrical power consumption," because one generation of eager consumers has already been born. That means more power plants will be built and more transmission lines strung; or put another way, more pollution.

The dangers of continued pollution are haunting the White House. In a June 1971 message to Congress outlining what purports to be a national energy policy, President Nixon used the word "clean" more times than a detergent commercial and pledged unspecified environmental safeguards in all his proposals—clearly indicating that electricity will become more expensive (nothing about environmental protection is cheap). There was little to object to in many of the president's proposals and much to applaud. Who could argue with the need to conserve energy by providing better insulation for buildings? Who could object to more research to find ways of removing sulfur from coal, or to the creation of a Natural Resources Department to "classify, express and execute federal energy policy?"

But when President Nixon proposed to expand the U. S.'s supply of fossil fuels by leasing additional federal lands on the outer continental shelf, former Secretary of the Interior Stewart Udall complained: "They still have not learned the lessons of the Santa Barbara oil spill." Another recommendation to extract oil from shale also angered critics, who know that it now takes 66,000 tons of shale to produce 52,500 barrels of not very good quality oil. And the only economical way to mine the shale is to tear off the topsoil with tremendous machines, then gouge out the greasy rock, leaving a landscape of lasting desolation. Conservationists will try to prevent these disasters.

Although the president made other, more welcome proposals for developing new technologies and sources of energy, critics doubt whether any of them will produce enough power to satisfy the nation in the near future. The Joint Congressional Committee on Atomic Energy was probably closer to the truth when it predicted that nuclear power plants would supply 25 percent of the U.S.'s electricity needs by 1980, 40 percent by 1990 and 60 percent by 2000. "I've always said that the environmental movement would end up driving the nation toward nuclear energy at an even faster pace," says Congressman Chet Holifield, the single most influential member of the Joint Committee. "The more the trade-offs are studied, the better atomic plants are going to look." How good is that? Let us follow Cal Tech's lead and assume the best: direct low-level radioactive and thermal emissions will be near-zero, safety features are perfected. But even then environmentalists are unlikely to accept the nukes without a continuous fight, for there remains the large problem of the reactors' high-level radioactive wastes.

There is only one way for radioactivity to dissipate from the waste product of a nuke—slowly. Some lethal radioactive elements like strontium-90 and cesium-137 have half-lives of decades. Plutonium-239, according to scientists' estimates, is hazardous for 500,000 years. These hot (600 degrees and up) wastes must be stored where they cannot leak into the biosphere for thousands of centuries; if the Pharaohs had buried them, they would still be deadly.

The AEC first proposed to create an atomic "tomb" in thick beds of salt deep under the pleasant farming town of Lyons, Kansas. Containerized wastes would be shipped by rail to Lyons from reprocessing plants, then be buried in vaults anywhere from 500 to 2,000 feet underground. Once the capacity of the vault had been reached (about twenty containers), the room would be refilled with loose salt. Within three years, the heat from the wastes would melt the steel and ceramic containers and eventually the surrounding salt as well. The AEC believes this molten salt will protect man indefinitely from his most deadly garbage.

While most of Lyons' 4,300 people apparently do not mind the idea of living over an atomic crypt, the Kansas Geological Survey and U.S. Interior Department are doing some profound worrying for them. One objection is that if something went wrong, the wastes would be extremely difficult to retrieve before they seeped into underground water supplies and out into the environment. Another problem is what the molten salt might do over the ages. Perhaps it would shift so that the overlying rocks would crack; or perhaps it would suddenly release its stored heat in muffled subterranean explosions. In either case, surface and ground water might percolate down to the salt and through the radioactive wastes. No one is sure.

Critics of the project include many Kansas state legislators and Representative Joe Skubitz. "How ironic it is," Skubitz told the Joint Committee, "for a congressman to sit here today and plead that an agency of government not pollute the environment while at the same time Congress will be asked to consider the expenditure of billions of dollars to clean up pollution that already exists. How ironic it is to be required to make a case against a new kind of pollution so hazardous and so lethal that all existing pollution seems almost inconsequential." To this, Representative Holifield replied that after fifteen years of study, a demonstration project was surely needed. Another nuclear booster on the Joint Committee, Representative Craig Hosmer, added: "I get the impression that we should never have invented the wheel if we had thought about it before hand."

When questioned about waste disposal problems, electric utility executives are ready with an answer: "Either you have faith in technology or you don't." *They* do. *Environmentalists* don't. The dangers of high-level radioactive wastes already figure in citizen interventions in several AEC-electric utility hearings. As of this writing, the AEC has dropped plans for storing the radioactive ashes in Kansas's salt mines—when flooded with water in a test, the Lyons "tomb" proved as leaky as a sieve—and is looking into other possible locations. Whatever the outcome, it seems clear that the problem will not go away in the future—at least not for 500,000 years.

There is another sure controversy on the horizon, though it is right now no bigger than a man's memory of a mushroom cloud. "Our best hope for meeting the nation's growing demand for electricity lies with the fast breeder reactor," President Nixon said in his energy message, indulging in a little boosterism himself. "Because of its highly efficient use of nuclear fuel, the breeder reactor would extend the life of our natural uranium resources from decades to centuries, with far less impact on the environment than the power plants which are operating today."

But such practical considerations do not appease environmentalists. The Scientists' Institute for Public Information (SIPI) argues that starting the breeder program, as the AEC and president want, will give it momentum which will be almost impossible to halt later on. Rather than wait, SIPI filed suit against the Atomic Energy Commission in May, 1971, asking that the AEC submit an adequate environmental impact statement on the proposed program. The scientists worry about high-level wastes, but particularly fear plutonium, which the suit describes as "one of the most explosive and toxic substances known to man."

Physicist Sidney J. Socolar of Columbia University, a SIPI member, warns that plutonium would cause cancer if it escaped into the environment. How might it escape? "A breeder reactor," he says, "would react to disturbance or overheating by the compaction of plutonium and acceleration of the nuclear reaction. The result might be a nuclear explosion." SIPI also mentioned that the breeder's coolant, liquid sodium, explodes when in contact with air or water.

No matter how small these risks may be, many people would prefer not to allow them to arise in the first place. If the price be a power shortage, they say, let there be brownouts and blackouts. What is obviously needed is a system of constraints on production and consumption of energy. But how does a free society arrive at such a reordering of priorities? The answer must be worked out, not in the privacy of board rooms, but in public, where such major decisions properly belong.

About the Sierra Club

The Sierra Club, founded in 1892 by John Muir, has consistently devoted itself to the study and protection of America's scenic resources and wild places. Sierra Club publications are part of the nonprofit effort the club carries on as a public trust. There are chapters in all parts of the United States. Participation is invited in the club's program to enjoy and preserve wilderness, wildlife, and a quality environment for all men, for all time.

Part of the club program aims to service the growing student environmental movement on the nation's campuses. Information on organizational techniques, eco-tactics and community action is available from The Campus Program, Sierra Club, Mills Tower, San Francisco, California 94104.

The Sierra Club
Mills Tower
San Francisco, California 94104

Please enroll me as a member of the Sierra Club:

Name_____

Address_____

City, state, zip_____

Dues: $5 admission, plus $15 (regular membership) , $7.50 (spouse) or $5 (full-time students, age 15 through 23) .

I enclose_____

(We must have this information if applicant is student)

Birthdate_____

School and location_____

Other Sierra Club Battlebooks

Clearcut The Deforestation of America, by Nancy Wood.
176 pages. 16 pages of black and white photographs. $2.75

Having overcut their own lands, timber companies now look increasingly to the national forests, where the bite of the chain saw already is fastened upon some of the last great stands of virgin timber in America. The loggers practice clearcutting. And in pursuit of this scalped land policy, they obliterate many of the other values—soil and watershed protection, wildlife habitat, recreation—that the national forests were established to sustain in perpetuity.

Clearcut examines this continuing raid on our forest resources and challenges both government and industry to provide, through forestry reform, a guarantee that America shall forever have wilderness as well as wood products.

Oilspill by Wesley Marx.   144 pages. $2.75

In 1970, an estimated 1.5 billion gallons of crude and bunker oil spilled into the oceans of the world from tankers and offshore wells. Nearly half of the major spills were within a mile of the shore. The toll in shellfish and seabirds, in lost recreational opportunities along miles of gummy beaches, in direct economic setbacks to the coastal communities affected will never be fully tabulated.

Oilspill reveals the full story of this increasing threat to our precious marine environments. Author Wesley Marx describes the ecological impact of spilt oil, the vulnerability of supertankers, the hazards of coastal refineries, the flaws in our fumbling technology for cleaning up after industry's mess. Marx also explores some new ideas that could help ease America off her hydrocarbon habit before the oceans are irrevocably fouled and oil replaces water as the most prominent fluid on this planet.

Oil On Ice by Tom Brown.   160 pages. $1.95

One of Alaska's foremost journalists explores a leading threat to the delicate ecosystem of our largest state, as the proposed oil pipeline controversy nears a final decision. The extraction of petroleum here might well inject new strength into Alaska's economy but it could just as easily upset the arctic's fragile environment if scalding oil is piped 800 miles from the North Slope to Valdez, over and under unstable permafrost soils and across earthquake fault zones. Brown presents his information objectively, leaving conclusions to the reader.

Mercury by Katherine and Peter Montague.   160 pages. $2.25

A startling, fresh account of how U.S. public health officials looked the other way while quicksilver infiltrated the food chains leading to man. As *The Los Angeles Times* noted: "The Montagues have written a sane, balanced and well-documented history... Its value is enhanced by the excellent end-of-the-book listings of polluters, polluting processes, state and federal legislation and a bibliography. Well worth the time of anyone concerned with the facts behind a current scare."